£1.50

St Kilda Diary

....

A Record of the
Early Re-Occupation of St Kilda

Dr David Boddington

D1615673

The Islands Book Trust

Published in 2010 by The Islands Book Trust

www.theislandsbooktrust.com

© David Boddington

ISBN: 978-0-9560764-5-8

British Library Cataloguing in Publication Data. A CIP record
for this book can be obtained from the British Library.

All rights reserved. No part of this publication may be
reproduced, stored in a retrieval system, or transmitted in
any other form or by any means, electronic, mechanical,
photocopying, recording or otherwise without the prior written
permission of the publishers. This book may not be lent, hired
out, resold or otherwise disposed of by way of trade in any form
of binding or cover other than that in which it is published,
without the prior consent of the publishers.

The Islands Book Trust would like to thank David Boddington and
John Love for their assistance with the production of this volume.

Line drawings © and courtesy of John Love
Front cover image © David Shepherd and courtesy of
the Ministry of Defence

The Islands Book Trust, Ravenspoint Centre, Kershader, South
Lochs, Isle of Lewis, HS2 9QA. Tel: 01851 880737

Typeset by Erica Schwarz. Printed by J F Print Limited, UK

The European Agricultural Fund
for Rural Development:
Europe investing in rural areas

The Scottish
Government
Riaghaltas na h-Alba

HIE
Innse Gall
Outer Hebrides

Contents

Glossary

....

LCT	Landing Craft Tank
RA	Royal Artillery
ETD	Expected Time Departure
ETA	Expected Time Arrival
NC	Nature Conservancy
RAMC	Royal Army Medical Corps
NAAFI	Naval Army Air Force Institution (an organisation supplying the Forces with canteen and shop facilities and other goods not coming under the heading of service goods and daily rations)
RASC	Royal Army Service Corps
NTS	National Trust for Scotland
MI Room	Medical Inspection Room
MO	Medical Officer
RT	Radio Transmission
ACC	Army Catering Corps
MOD	Ministry of Defence
RAF	Royal Air Force
WO	Warrant Officer
SOC	Scottish Ornithological Club
REME	Royal Electrical & Mechanical Engineers
RSM	Regimental Sergeant Major
NO	Nursing Orderly
OC	Officer Commanding

Q	Quartermaster
RAOC	Royal Army Ordinance Corps
DDMS	Deputy Director Medical Services
WT	Wireless & telephone
BTO	British Trust for Ornithology
QARANC	Queen Alexandra's Royal Army Nursing Corps
AQMS	Assistant Quartermaster Sergeant
NVC	National Vegetation Classification
DRF	Directional Range Finder
OTC	Officer Training Corps
Scot. Co.	Scottish Command
RE	Royal Engineers
EUOTC	Edinburgh University Officer's Training Corps
POL	Fuel oil
'Chippy'	Carpenter

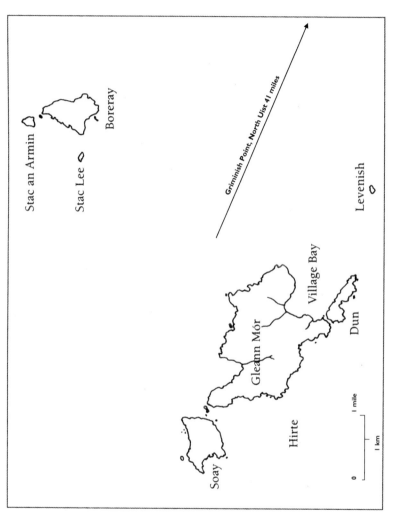

MAP 1. *The Islands of St Kilda*

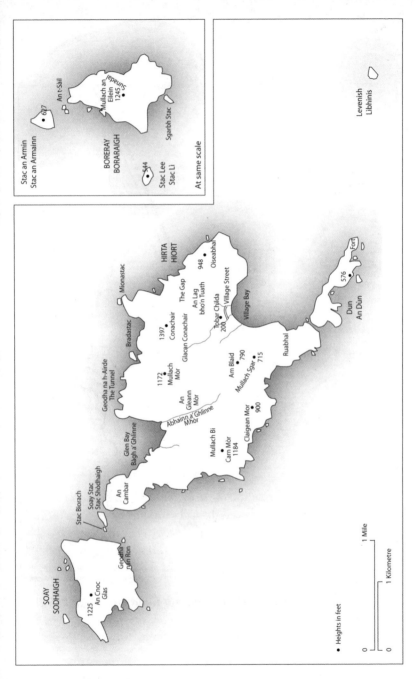

MAP 2. *Main Place-Names Mentioned in Book*

Introduction

....

Herring Gull and Chick

This section was written during my first week on Hirta at the end of August 1958, and in retrospect would be as appropriate now as it was then. Any commentary needed is in different type, and few alterations have been made, but omissions have been made for reasons of space or repetition. Latin nomenclature and post 1959 knowledge acquired are in italics also.

From the start the Diaries were to be an account of my activities and those of the Unit, and more especially my own responsibilities within the Unit and those delegated to me as Nature Conservancy Warden and representative of the National Trust for Scotland. They were not intended to be for bird records. These have been kept separate in my own smaller book, and in a log book provided by the NC. My own letters home were kept by the family and have been used here.

My own intention as a serving soldier to stick to the 50 year rule has been met, and apart from a number of lectures, my first release to the press was when I was invited by The Islands Book Trust to talk in 2008 at an event they organised to mark the end of the initial stage of Operation Hardrock in 1958: 50 years from when the RAF team started it.

Such are the minds of men that they constantly seek the future and the past, even though contented with the present; the heights and depths, though neither are environmentally suitable; isolation and hardship though company and comfort are amongst the great attributes of our species.

For those that have at some time chosen these paths there may have been guides, but as often as not there was nothing to guide the way. St Kilda was certainly not unplotted, anyhow from the seventeenth century onwards, and even after the spartan existence of the inhabitants became unbearable in their minds and illogical in the minds of others, resulting in evacuation, the call of such far lands needed no resisting and men returned to see, enquire and record.

A chance remark by a friend in a hospital corridor originated the idea, and a love of islands fostered it. Its 'incubation' was long, continually checked for progress, several times nearly ended, and once prematurely almost seen to a successful conclusion. However the intention being to include as many months as possible on the island, at the same time as completing an obligatory two years Army service, was for ever in my mind. Indeed it was on paper in the War Office, but was so poorly appreciated in Scottish Command that they could only give me two days warning.

Two days in which to prepare for a year's absence is not long, and even though it eventually became four, seemed little longer. But with the anticipation that soon an obsession would be fulfilled there was no grief. Indeed how could there be, knowing that I was to be the first naturalist to remain on St Kilda during the winter, and therefore have great opportunities to solve problems and fill a seasonal gap in knowledge for the first time.

DAVID BODDINGTON

Grey Seal Underwater

Chapter One

....

Storm Petrel Head

August 25, 1958 – The Departure

'Alpha and Omega, the beginning and the end'. Both were uncertain but today Alpha can at least be referred to as part of the past, for at 15.45 hours LCT 4074 slowly emerged from under the giant electric cranes on the wharf at Cairnryan harbour on the way to St Kilda.

I had spent the previous two nights at the Loch Ryan Hotel at the entrance to the Royal Pioneer Corps base, having driven down with Sinclair, the Cowglen Military Hospital Officers' Mess steward, on the Saturday, in quite glorious sunshine, along the Clyde coast. During the evening we had an excellent dinner at the George Hotel and later went on to a village hop at Port Patrick, a sweet little village, quite unspoilt, and overlooking Ireland across St George's Channel. Tommy left with my car on the Sunday morning and I spent the rest of the day quietly in the Officers' Mess.

This morning I was driven by service vehicle to the pier and 4074 was coming towards us from Stranraer. The skippers were given considerable liberty as to where they spent non sailing time and this enabled the crew to 'see life' at week-ends. 4074 was a 1000Ton Tank Landing Craft which had been in cocoons until 1956 and was now being used to service the Guided Weapons Range, the main base being on South Uist and Benbecula. These vessels were 250ft long and grey all over, with the first 180ft for a low deck cargo which could be driven out of the bow doors when the craft was beached.

'Aft' she had a bridge with wheelhouse underneath and behind this was the officer's sleeping quarters and Ward Room, all of which were comfy with dunlopillow beds. Below this was the troops' quarters and lower still the diesel engines. The Captain was a second Lieut. Peter Jones, and the crew were RASC lads, most of who were on National Service. There was a Decca Radar navigation system which could be preset. I boarded at 08.15 hours and was met in the Ward Room by Lieut. Col. George Cooper RA, attached to the War Office and well versed with the situation, and Dr Morton Boyd of the Nature Conservancy who was visiting for a week. This was a lucky meeting for me and the NC offered to supply me with film and scientific equipment, which was gratifying.

ETD was post-lunch in order to get the evening tide in Village Bay, so I took Morton off to leave his car at the Officer's Mess garage and we got back for lunch. The ETD was altered to coincide with the arrival of NAAFI stores loaded into two trailers, and the addition of a 3-toner, and we cast off at 15.45 hours. The sea was calm and we made 10 knots out of the harbour with the sun on the hills around, a straight white wake behind us, and numerous gulls overhead. By 18.00 we had made 16.6 sea miles, the Mull of Kintyre ahead, the coast of Ireland to our left and Ailsa Craig sticking up boldly to our right: all was peaceful save for the hum of the generators and engines. We passed the Mull of Kintyre at 19.30 hours about 3 miles off it, where rafts of Manx Shearwaters gathered prior to their dusk flight to land. The white lighthouse with a few clustered houses stood lone and defiant at the cliff base with the green sward above seeming to vanish into orographic cloud, which hung, moving and yet still, in smooth silky wisps over the top.

At 20.00 hours we passed the Mull and were continuing our course so to pass Islay. The Paps of Jura were far away to our right, and the clouds here only hid their shoulders, leaving the masses of the rocky peaks to protrude upwards uncovered.

The wind was f. 1–2 and the sea just ruffled. For some time I stood on the bow watching the 'tubenoses', with the sun ahead just starting to go red and a yet pale moon coming up behind us. At 20.15 hours an Arctic Skua flew across the bow when we were about 37 miles out from Cairnryan, and less than an hour later I was photographing the dying sun prior to my own 'setting' to bed. Once in bed the moon glistened across the water behind us and some Irish Lights flashed intermittently.

August 26

As the day started we had just completed 74.6 miles, and at 04.00 hours, just off Skerryvore in a SSW f. 3 wind, we had covered 113.8 miles. On waking at 08.30 hours, feeling very refreshed, we had covered 156 miles. The sky was overcast and the warm front that had appeared impending as high *cirrus* clouds last evening, was now on us. Behind to the right were the Outer Hebrides and their southern end, Barra

Head. Somewhere straight ahead lay St Kilda. There was a thin mist and after a coffee in the Ward Room I emerged to see a Great Shearwater about twenty yards away, and a Meadow Pipit pausing on deck. The nearest land, the Monach Isles, were 20 miles away and South Uist, 25. It was raining a little and visibility was down to ten miles or less. An *Alba* Wagtail appeared. The frontal conditions were causing disorientation in the small birds whose migratory urge had been stimulated by the high pressure behind us.

Soon after, at 11.30 hours, I emerged again to get my first view of the island which was going to be my home for some months ahead. It was a misty view but threateningly impressive with Stac Li and Boreray away to the right, and Hirta, the main mass with the village bay just visible in the centre into which we were heading; but before we got in I was to get a big surprise.

August 26 (cont.) – The Arrival

A new trawler which had been on our starboard side for a few minutes suddenly started flashing her Aldis lamp. I was down below at the time and when Morton came down and said that a doctor was wanted, thought he was being cheerful, however it was so, and the trawler was instructed to follow us in, which it did (*name was* Velia *FD 116*).

It was 14.00 hours when we started to enter the bay guided by two strong yellow lights, and the landing place upon which we hoped to beach the boat later in the day after high tide at 15.42 hours was directly under these. However it was soon apparent that if the sea got any rougher there would be no landing at all, and if the wind remained at SE f. 4–5, which it had been for an hour, an increase in the sea would be probable (*blowing directly into the bay*). Soon the stern anchor was down and the ship swung pendulum like in the wind. The trawler was now near but would come no nearer than 150 to 200 yards, and as the dory boat was being swung over the side of the LCT, I put on my Mae West and inflated it. The dory was bouncing up and down the side of the ship and I lowered myself down the rope ladder, choosing the opportune moment to drop into the boat as it rose momentarily towards me. It was 12ft long with a crew of four and myself in the stern and they pulled the boat slowly towards the trawler. At one point a rowlock broke but it was soon replaced, and after what seemed like 10 minutes but was probably 5, we were alongside.

Once again the boat jumped up hard against the ship, and when the roll was right I threw up my arms towards the rail and was hauled up head first onto the deck, the battery on my jacket falling onto the floor. The crew followed and while the boat vanished from my sight as it was tied astern, I was led up to the skipper who took me into a snug softly furnished lounge. On the right hand side was the Chief Engineer who complained of deafness and pain in his right ear. Without an auriscope I felt a little lost, but he had an ear full of wax and some lymphadenitis or phlebitis behind it at a site that a vein leads directly into the brain.

The medicine chest contained a 'sulfa' drug (*sometime called M&B when it was first discovered in the 1930s*) and the skipper said that they had had penicillin, but the crew used them as sleeping tablets. Directions were left and serious signs to look out for were written down. The boat came alongside and in we dropped. Once the oars were in we drew off. This time we were broadside to the waves, and fearing to foul the stern anchor we went around the bow to get to the starboard side. Once there we caught a line but it was some minutes before we could get amidships owing to the huge waves coming down the side of the vessel. Constantly we were thrown against it and I feared for the hands of the lads as they tried to keep us off, preferring a smashed gunwale to a pulped hand. Each wave seemed bigger than the rest and we were getting wet, but after getting to the ladder I bade my time for the right moment to cling onto it and hauled myself up eight foot until I got my head as far as the deck, legs dangling behind. I was told later that they grabbed one thigh and one arm, and it was like pulling a large wet slippery halibut on board.

It was now 15.10 hours and I rested in the Ward Room. The wind blew more, and with a flowing tide, the sea got bigger. It was clear we were not going to be able to beach, and there was talk of running 60 miles with the wind to shelter behind South Uist, but Morton Boyd suggested we went around to Glen Bay away from the SE wind, on the NW corner of the island, an area as yet uncharted but where he knew trawlers had sought shelter. So with the mist coming down we weighed anchor and went anti-clockwise around the island to reach the comparative calm of Glen Bay near the highest cliffs on the island. From these, gusts of fierce wind, announcing their advent with rushing ferocity cut the tops of the waves into white flashing streaks, spraying water into the air.

Without the shuddering of the ship we had experienced while off the village we felt safer, and there was less danger of dragging our anchor here. We dropped our stern anchor 100 yards off shore, pulled up on it, and released the bow anchor. After soup and toast I went to bed at 21.00 hours.

August 27

It was blowing even harder at 09.00 hours, the warm front had failed to move on, the cold front arrived at 17.00 hours, the wind fell to f. 4 with a clear sky above our local stratus. Temptation to go round to Village Bay was resisted in case failure and return meant anchoring in the dark. Two people landed from the dory, handed over Royal Mail to two soldiers who needed to carry it over 900ft to the hut. Soundings showed up to 23 fathoms at 30 yards from the cliffs.

August 28

Awakening to hear the wind still whistling around the decks I did not have much hope of leaving our safe seclusion. The squalls were even more wicked than yesterday and the sea was still being ruffled out of an acceptable benign state. However during the morning we pulled up both anchors and then pushed out of our hiding place at 10 knots towards the island of Boreray, about 4 miles off, an isle that looked frighteningly majestic with a crown of cloud to befit it. A SE wind of about f. 6 strength whipped the tops off the swell which we were trying to turn into. The design of the craft enabled the bow to twist one way and the stern the other: a feature causing comfort if you thought about it, but alarm to see it happening. This 15 degree roll together with the plunging pitch of near 17 degrees and water that broke over us in spite of the fact that we had partial shelter still, persuaded us to return to Glen Bay.

The wind started to veer westerly in the evening and we radioed our intention to try at midnight. Time started to drag. Morton slept and others read but there was no suggestion of concentration. Not even hot tea helped. Soon we were all up; that is except for two cases of influenza down below.

Bow anchor party assembled and pulled up a tardy weight which had been dragged along the sea bed at 25 fathoms for the last 12 hours as a means of preventing us swinging while the stern anchor held us, and then the stern anchor party started their rather harder job. The winch creaked and groaned, with a hawser bent twice before it finally turned towards its goal, and the Navigation Officer and Captain flitted from stern to bridge ready to ring for full ahead when the ship was free. The full moon was half hidden when the engines drove us ahead, but there was enough light for visual navigation to get us out of the bay, and we slowly emerged and turned starboard well clear of Conachair and Oiseval, realising how much the sea had gone down. The RT operator below kept in touch with the boarding party and a signaller with a lamp was ready on the bridge. Ramsay, a thick set sailor of few words, who had helped pull me onto the boat two days ago, stood at the wheel repeating back the orders given by the Captain.

It looked hopeful, and soon after the twinkling lights on the buoys became visible, appeared a yellow orange glow from two arc lights set higher up the beach to guide us in. With these in line we slowly crept in, getting increasing shelter from the SW wind. The Aldis lamps were flashing from ship to shore, and shore to ship. My baggage was on top inside the 3 ton lorry, and that would be followed by two tractors and trailers. Men were to come off and men to go on. Men were around the two front opening doors loosening the ramp. Figures could be seen on shore outlined against the orange lights behind. The moon appeared for a moment, quite full, as if eager to be the sole witness of problems to come; nocturnal, post 48 hour gale and a tide just about to ebb. This meant that it could momentarily turn on us at any time before really retreating. The senior officer sat in the front of the 3 toner and I chose to sprawl across the top of the luggage in his lorry. A Sgt. RASC started up our engine and drove down the ramp. Both sets of wheels fell into about a foot of water and the engine stalled. Water was soon at floor level for Colonel and driver, and after a pull from the tractor up the beach his exit coincided with a tide surge designed to seek out seniority. I was dry. I walked up the now soft churned up sand towards the group of figures at the top of the track leading to the area at the top of the beach. Major 'Topper' Brown, the RAMC Quartermaster at Cowglen hailed me, still wearing the full service dress he had left Glasgow in, in spite of my warning that if it was St Kilda he had suddenly been asked to visit, not to bother with his smart hat (*he left the Military Hospital, Cowglen with two days warning and a negligent briefing, on 'taking over' from the RAF, unaware that he had to cross the sea. Showing him the pictures in Lonely Islands by Roland Svensson were too dramatic for his level of belief*). I signed unread papers he held out, and sent regards to his wife who, he tells me, did not know where he was.

Soon Jonah's Whale was ready to swallow up a group of officers, 20 other rank pioneers, two Land Rovers, and two empty trailers, all of which were pulled up through 3ft of water well into the vehicle deck by the bulldozer tractor inside. The whole job took an hour from when we landed at 01.15 hours. Her hunger satisfied, she closed up her bow end and reversed engines to pull herself out into the darkness. The moon had seen it all and was clouded over; we were all happy to be on land, soon warmed with soup and there was no better way to finish the day when Dr Sandy Bruce, a transient helper, brought me 7 Storm Petrels and a Leach's Petrel in a bag to ring in my pyjamas.

CHAPTER TWO

....

Long Tailed Field Mouse

August 29 – Setting up and settling down

After breakfast my Sergeant and Private RAMC met me outside the Mess to introduce me to the MI room just around the corner. This was going to be the Medical Centre. It was a converted Nissen hut (*which had been put together during the previous winter by Flying Officer, later Flight Lieut., Peter Saundby and his medical staff*) with a covered porch which led into a reception room 12ft wide and 16ft long. Swing doors to the right led into a six bedded ward. The two rooms on the left would be Treatment and Operative, and Laboratory and Diagnostic. The latter room would double up as a bird ringing room. During the day we sorted out most of the very lavish equipment and drugs left to us by the RAF (*some years later*

I met up with Dr Saundby. He had later reached the rank of Air Commodore and worked in Tri-service operations at the MOD with logistics, and remembers that then the demands of army medical services were always the least of the three. There seemed to be a clear tactical reason for this).

August 30

Wind SW f. 8 all day. Photography from opposite the Island of Dun which gives protection of the bay from the west. (*I had an old Voigtlander Vito B given to me by my CO at Cowglen without lens attachments).*

August 31

Sunday today. Not quite a working day, the lads having the afternoon off were occupied from 11.00 hours in the morning watching a fire fighting demonstration. A brilliantly fine day with a placid sea in the bay, so I did some washing and hung it out to dry.

A fully fledged Fulmar Petrel was brought in with a flail leg fractured above the tibio-tarsal joint. Amputation was decided and I gave it nitrous oxide from our Boyles apparatus. We gave it enough to prevent any acute pain. A spurting artery was a good sign and we applied cotton wool and collodion as a dressing. The bleeding stopped and it had a return to the box being fed later on sardine oil squirted in with a syringe. Later on the mackerel close to the edge of the shore were taking evasive action from the seals, semi-emerging from the water, but thereby exposing themselves to the exited diving gannets close to us. There was 'play' showing in the eyes of the seals and 'fear' in the eyes of the fish. Oh for a net and a boat. The gannets are probably keen to get a final feed after their main feeding journey to the Minch, around Barra Head or through the Sound of Harris 60 to 90 miles away. At this feed the load was such that many had difficulty in flying off (*nine months later I was able to* watch *a gannet emerging from the water with difficulty from amongst escaping mackerel with the nose of a seal amongst its feathers*).

September 1

Sandy Bruce awoke me in my tiny temporary room just before 08.00 hours to say the boat was in, and it was lying off shore. There was to be an early lunch anticipating the craft beaching at noon. An Army Catering Corps WO 2 landed and will be staying 2 weeks. Morton was due to go off as was Captain Bruce, who decided to change into a smart grey suit (!) but intended to retain his beard. When the empty trailers were loaded we went aboard for tea. This craft had a more naval atmosphere about it than 4074. The Skipper was a relaxed semi retired naval man still sailing big and small boats with distinction.

The three Skippers I met were competent and wisely relied on the 2nd in charge where problems might arise. 4074 had a Skipper of 22 who stated at his entry interview that he intended to be a BA pilot and liked sailing. When it came to our movements on arrival I witnessed the close liaison between him and his older WO (first mate).

At about 17.00 hours I heard the plaintive sound of pipes from the bridge as she departed, and being an ex huntsman of Beagles blew 'going home' on my hunting horn. Going they were. I explored Oiseval with a spiralling climb to the summit of 948ft where I was joined by a pair of ravens, and three swifts feeding in the E to NE wind at c. 700ft. Just two of us, Major Riach RA and myself for supper and it was to be two for sometime.

September 2

This morning I made an attack on my drug cupboard sorting out all the drugs into a sensible pharmacological order (*when I later went into a rural dispensing General Practice in Herefordshire I repeated the performance*). In the afternoon I took up Private Rhodes RAMC to my new room at the top of the Factor's House, to help lay my carpet. Then between us we did a great amount of bashing on the chest of drawers to get the drawers free. He, with an engineering qualification, had an advantage over me both in the appraisal of the situation and the mode of attack. If either of us had injured ourselves there was no fear for he was a Nursing Officer with a few months training. We then went to our first patient on the island, Charles the fulmar petrel. He had been on sea water drinks but had not swallowed voluntarily (*I later discovered that most Petrels leave the nest well 'fatted' in the expectation of not feeding for some days*).

He had a sea water bath and some tilting exercises: so many perfect reflexes to alter body position according to the air currents. Soon he started a long glide down from the Gap at 700ft to Village Bay, with the wind behind, and I watched him for half a mile (one cannot sex them at that age!). A fit bird I would have thrown high and fast into the wind. I climbed into a position from where I could examine the SE facing cliff of Conachair which is about 1100ft high. Even from 800ft the fulmars on the sea below were merely white specks. There were plenty of young birds on the cliff nests, with mature and younger mature adults all making competitive noises for a ledge even for next year. I took a sheep path 30ft down, but thought better and sat. Away on Boreray 4 miles to the NE I could just pick out individual gannets looking like barnacles on a rock face, and beyond was Stac Li, 544ft, and Stac an Armin, a mile further on, 627ft. Overhead were thousands of white adult gannets, the young being brown. I started back at 18.15, covering the half mile in twelve minutes, and going by An lag Bho'n Tuath saw evidence of ridges and small platforms.

September 3

A fine sunny day which persisted with only a vestige of wind in the bay but with a strong SE'er up top; and it was up there that I was to go after lunch. There was a long sinuous road past the quarry to Am Blaid, a relatively flat area at 700ft, overlooking Gleann Mor and Glen Bay, where we had sheltered, to the north. I explored the surrounds of the Decca Radar set on Ruaival on which I hoped later to do research on flight patterns of sea-birds, and then moved north to Mullach Bi, 1164ft. From this rocky crag it would be possible to go down the slope to the NE to the centre of Gleann Mor, and with a safely chosen detour, down to Carn Mor to the SW, where is the large colony of Manx Shearwaters, Storm Petrels, and Leach's Forked Tailed Petrels.

I did discover the way down during the next hour: as a future guide I placed a piece of aeroplane wreckage (a small wheel 6 inches in diameter) just inside a cleit in the boundary wall on the right. This is the last good cleit before Mullach Bi, and it is here that one goes down the grassy slope to the left (west), past a wrecked cleit, and further down still until one gets to a shoulder high buttress on the right where one carefully climbs around the bottom onto a boulder strewn slope up which on the talus it is easier and safer to climb at an angle upwards.

It is a world of its own down here, but having found it there was a need to leave it as I was due to finish the blood letting session which I had started that morning, at 16.30 hours. My climb back got me up to the path to Mullach Bi at 16.15 hours, and leaving the high crags to my left I turned right, and with the help of some athleticism from the top of Am Blaid to the village street, I was back hot and bedraggled at 16.45 hours for my session; the purpose being to have everyone's blood group and Rhesus factor identified at Cowglen. The boat was due tomorrow and they would return with the samples.

For fear it might appear that the whole day was spent at play, let it be noted that I wrote to the DDMS (Deputy Director General of Medical Services) in the morning and also finished off my drug cupboard. Its order is now consistent with my lines of therapeutic thought.

As if to show approval the aurora borealis displayed before bed.

September 4

The LTC had left Benbecula at 11.00 hours and was expected here around 18.00 hours, so spirits were high during the day and further heightened by fine weather. Wrote during the morning but as the ETA was changed to 01.00 hours tomorrow the lads were given the afternoon off.

The day's activities included some attempt to Mist net some birds, and a trip up to the Decca for the two Sergeants and myself organised by Tony Riach. The four wheel drive one toner took all the slopes well, the worst road incline being one in three. No wonder it only does three miles to the gallon.

The view from the Marconi set on the top of Conachair was panoramic but sufficiently hazy to be confined to the island group. On our way back Tony dropped me at the bottom and I walked back along the village street. While finishing supper the boat came and tied up to the buoy in the bay. A Colonel from War House and an Intelligence Corps Captain were due to come off for a quick inspection. We could see they were smart so suggested that the less well clothed soldiers on the pier hid.

Tony took the senior officer up top and I took the Captain around the huts. It was dusk when we got back and the Col. asked me enough questions to occupy half an hour while we were having drinks in the Sergeant's Mess. The idea was to get opinions from all the soldiers but I am sure any grumbles will be made with light hearts and minds. Eventually I dragged the Col. outside to the best 'aurora' I had ever seen, the green and crimson folds surging from side to side like belly dancers. We could easily have been on the Riviera with the Onassis yacht in the bay. The boat came off the mooring and went out a short way to turn and start her run-in. We all went to the beach and she came in at 02.00, but did not drop her ramp for half an hour though the officers both watched proceedings with inquiring minds. They seemed duly impressed with our needs (*but later we were to wonder at the reasons from even higher why our requests were unreasonable*).

A fine example of *Apodemus sylvaticus hirtensis*, a subspecies or race of our mainland type, entered the room through the door left open in my absence. Its perambulation started around 04.00 hours and was firstly doing circuits of the room which included my pillow, and then up my leg between two blankets. I did not move. Still semi-comatose a little later it sat on my pillow so close that on opening my eyes it was out of focus. I opened the door!

September 5

The simple activities of the day included an extra half hour in bed, a late start in the Centre, an acceptance of the bacteriological report on the drinking water tested at Cowglen Hospital. As expected it had a high 'coliform' count due to contamination from sheep; the chlorine level – nil: an inspection was carried out. I had a bath and washed Glasgow out of my hair. Examination of two Spanish trawlers suggested that their lack of response to any message meant they were probably swapping crew (some spent the whole winter up here – illegal) and fish.

September 6

Much rain, after backing from S to NE. I made a Red Cross Flag. Boat expected at noon tomorrow.

September 7

Sunday. Heavy rain during the night. Sunny most of the day. I ringed two puffins that had been found in the generator sheds in the morning.

The young puffin is deserted by its parents when it starts to lose its down. Mainly by running it goes downhill in the dark avoiding some predation. The nesting hole is long and dark and it seeks such cover. In the Faroe Isles the puffin was important in their diet, and its population is 'nursed' when low. When the juveniles are being found in the harbour surrounds, the children are encouraged to take the young down to the harbour and throw them in ... and be late for school!

When these birds were taken by me – two hands and facing the sea – they got exited when about 80 yards away. When placed on the water they took a drink, and the mere dipping of the head brought the wings and feet into diving movements, and under they went with a succession of 10 second dives.

The boat arrived at 11.00 hours when I had a patient on the carpet with an epistaxis (nosebleed), but did not beach until 15.00 hours. The boat landed meat and three large fire foam machines: parentage was without doubt a brass Canon X Penny Farthing bicycle.

September 8

Some of the lads were 'suffering something terrible' from the
effects of the party last night. I had tasted the punch and it was
not very surprising. With the flag finished yesterday I worked
on the flagpole today and had it fixed with the flag up by lunch
time. Sun at lunchtime but otherwise dull all day with no wind.
After tea had great fun chasing a sedge warbler in the iris beds,
eventually catching it in a net the first time. It took exception
to the possibility of being an in patient in the medical centre
and did a self discharge through the door.

September 9

The first job this morning was a bold effort by all three medical
men to understanding the science of water pumping engines
in order to get the water pump working in the chlorinating
system. Our brains tussled with stroke lengths, stroke volumes,
cubic inches and other such units, and when our brains had
failed Rhodes and I put slide rules and logs to full use. Having
eventually got the answers, we failed to get it to start. To allow
ourselves one success in the day we got the Mountain Rescue
equipment out. We understood most of it but failed in finding
the correct method of slinging the stretcher, so decided to
contact the Unit at RAF Kinloss.

Official letters in the afternoon and then some time on the
pier with Tony Riach watching an adult Slavonian Grebe who
played with our observational techniques while it was washing
about eight yards away. Later it slept on the water unconcerned
by Bombardier Harris who was 'doing a Cliveden' when his
line went adrift in the sea. Not a lady in sight!

September 10

Today was not busy, but it was eventful. I did two dental examinations and took blood from the five newcomers to the island. The anaesthetic apparatus is now useable with ether or nitrous oxide.

After tea I made another try to go around Oiseval, the 948ft hill behind our hut and to the east of it. All the sheep paths are much the same. Even when using them it was necessary to lean on the inner hand as it was a very short maritime sward and when it wasn't probably one should not be there, because the sheep considered it too dangerous and it became a long Fescue sward. With crags above and circling fulmars on and around the ledges, wrens having lost their alarm call due to absence of predators, and using a song instead, contrast was the only word to use. A small group of Soay sheep chose to break past me rather than move on: an ominous sign for safety: I returned the same way back for supper.

A strange ship appeared four miles out, headed into the bay, looked at us, refused to answer signals, and vanished off to the NW: probably an Iron Country Depot ship. Tony and I went up top to check she was not going to send a party ashore in Glen Bay. We both celebrated our findings at the Canteen Bar. Having decided to go to Carn Mor at about midnight I agreed to meet Bombardier Harris at 22.30 hours in the canteen and we set off fully equipped up the road reaching the top of Am Blaid in 28 minutes. The sky was clear but it seemed likely that mist would come soon and I took double precautions about checking up on navigating points for the return trip. Carn Mor was 1.25 miles away, but there were climbs at both ends, so I left plenty of time. At 23.35 hours I was looking for the marked cairn near Mullach Bi which would indicate to us when to start down the grassy slope. Down below the seals wailed. I was carrying two long bamboo poles with nets attached so that a series of balancing acts were needed in going down the long wet grassy slope, but we eventually got down and went around the buttress onto the boulder strewn face. There were a few petrels flying over and I heard the first shearwater calling away to our left. We sat and listened to the silence without torches (*as the vikings would have in the Scottish Isles perplexed to the point of fear*). We ringed a few birds and made our way back to the buttress, starting the climb back to 800ft and feeling relieved at the top to find only moderate mist. We stuck to the edge of the cliff making it safer navigationally but a little further, but then found the signal wire going to the Decca set. The stars and hilly points were invisible. At the opportune moment we left the line and struck off for the road, finding it exactly where the road down to the village branched off. The stars became visible and we covered the journey down in a quarter of an hour arriving back at 02.15 hours. Three long walks with different problems in 24 hours.

September 11

The boat was expected at 16.30 hours but did not arrive until 20.00 hours, when it came straight onto the beach. A fine day and after tea took a rather hesitant Sgt. Larham RAMC a short way around Oiseval to look for the boat. I wrote a letter home.

September 12

Answered some of yesterday's mail and carried out remedial surgery on my chest of drawers. Pt. Rhodes and myself started on the maths and design of our Ena Gyp rain gauge, which is a gadget made out of half a Gypsona plaster of Paris tin, and half an enema syringe. A graph was made to facilitate the interpretation. The Army had failed to agree about the hand over of some climatological equipment as it was not on any army list.

September 13

Enagyp was set up this morning with some protective wire around. Some room tidying this morning. Tony Riach and I are still continuing to 'tuck into' the stinking Camembert cheeses which arrived in the mail bag on the boat. Tony had sent to Fortnum and Mason for them. The boat journey had 'started them off' and the mail bag meaning to be always within the Skipper's sight and reach, was put on deck. Had it not contained our sovereign's Royal Mail it would have been hung overboard.

At 14.00 hours I set off for Gleann Mor, but the weather persisted fine and I headed for Mullach Bi and circled around the Gleann anti-clockwise until the far western end took me down into the bowl and I crossed it west to east up to its circular bank, which was obviously the remains of a stone wall banked up with soil, the ground being higher on the outside than on the inside. Back at the camp at 18.15 hours.

I have included in my diary details of the building remains found in the bottom of the bowl. I knew about these from Ken Williamson, and he with great knowledge of the buildings found in the Faeroes, had asked my opinion from slides he had shown at an SOC Meeting. What I saw today took me half way to my hypothesis which is explained later in these diaries.

September 14

Sunday. I rose at 09.15. The boat was lying at anchor in the bay, but did not beach until 10.45 hours, and even then she was not dry until an hour later. *Note the comfy difference between their landing and ours.* There was much mail to go through and I only finished at lunch time. There was a letter from Ken Williamson who I had first met on Fair Isle in 1955 making suggestions as to what work I might do here, a letter from Morton Boyd at the NC Edinburgh briefing me about the Spanish trawlers, and one from Dr Joe Eggeling appointing me as the Nature Conservancy's official representative on the island. Also a letter from Dad and some film from Agfa.

The low spring tide had exposed some new marine flora and fauna. I temporarily collect a fine urchin, *Echinus esculentius.* Tony and I had coffee on the LCT and the Skipper told me of a miniature wreck of Pipits they had had the previous night while 25 miles NW of Barra Head. This was interesting in view of the build up of Meadow Pipits there had been around the village.

September 15

Today arrived a table for my Sergeant, a fine desk for me and an examination couch for the treatment room. The REME RSM gave me a lift up the top to the cloud which was flowing fast up the west cliffs into Glen Mor and out again up the slope to the highest point, Mullach Mor, 1172ft, on which stood the Marconi Radar set, the larger of the two. A small flock of calling Lapland Buntings were seen flying in the stratus cloud. The habitat there would be familiar.

I made my way down Conachair's SE talus slope to the village, passing Tobar Childa and into the Village Street. A Manx Shearwater was the only patient in the MI room.

It was released on the sea but later returned to the pier and 'applied' for re-admission. I am now using 'live Longworth traps' to catch mice. Their release is publicly announced so that those with cameras can lie on the ground awaiting the emergence of the prisoner. After a short 'think' it takes a deliberate somersaulting run leaving the admirers facing several directions and rather frustrated. More puffins to ring.

September 16

I got the mist net up early and was soon catching Meadow Pipits. Even the two NOs remarked how different they seemed from the few resident ones we had had. One remarked on the darkness and one on their breasts, 'almost like a Robin'. An exaggeration but there was an overall darker hue and a crimson one also. They were birds of the western population which breeds in Iceland, the Faeroes and SE Greenland (*later established as A. pratensis whistleri*). This was assumed to be a local build up around the huts, but counts up top in the afternoon, made in a series of transects convinced me that there was probably a Hirta population of 7500 birds. So clear was the day that I could see a length of the Hebrides from Barra Head to the waves breaking on the Monach Isles.

September 17

The Pipits were still with us but last evening's kind easterly breeze had veered SE f. 5. This evening was the first with nothing to catch up on, so I listened to a Bach Prom which included 'Wachet auf' and the Double Violin Concerto. Two Spanish trawlers came in in the evening but left before midnight.

September 18

I wore my best khaki trousers because I had washed the others on the day before. The wind still blew and it was obvious that the boat would not start today. Bombardier Harris offered to take me and another up to the Marconi. The three of us in the back of the one toner were being asked to hold seven fire extinguishers to prevent the bumpy drive setting them off. So blowy at the top that to prevent being blown over one preferred to sit on the ground. Back to camp at 15.15 after a wet face stinging walk. Two birds in sick bay overnight.

Tony Riach was an ex Ack Ack gunner and with a small team of that ilk decided to do a test fire of three to spot the Radar splashes. Firing was to be at a bearing of 200 degrees, elevation 35 degrees, range 10,000 yards. They were 6ft long and weighed 140lbs: a small man load. The first was a misfire, and once the detonators had exploded there was melting of the metal present. The second was fired without any more success, but the third produced a premature swoosh and it was on its way. Just under a minute later I saw with my binocs, a 12ft splash, and what is more important, the Decca Radar recorded it. Mist netted after lunch, listened to Beethoven's 9th The Choral Symphony after supper and then went for drinks in the Sergeants' Mess at the Manse.

September 20

Weather too bad for the boat even to start. I got some late PM walking in.

September 21

Sunday. A rest day. I rose at 09.00 hours, had a leisurely breakfast, and listened to the wireless. Then a period of reading. Since coming I have caught up on years of leisure reading from the library that the RAF left behind. The least enjoyable has been one by J.B.Priestley: was it Angel Steps: and the most

Lorna Doone, suitable for the book list of male adolescents. While a medical student, all time was rationed out. There were oral and written exams for two years, then two years of depending on your own motivation and vocation, watched by your seniors, then two lots of finals with self organised revision, then the pass or fail, or retake, then two junior hospital posts which in my case involved much night work, then National Service. Sorry Priestley! Fitted into this had to come exercise, hobbies, and gentle courting without any involvement. I did a two mile walk in the evening and this enabled one pastoral act; the freeing of a still angry Soay tup from 20 yards of free running telephone line around its horns and hind legs. Not quite up to Daniel in the Lion's Den!

September 22

It was a fine day, but only from the point of the weather, because when extracting Sgt. Larham's painful tooth in the morning, the crown broke off. I had done 22 at Cowglen without mishap, partly my fault but not helped by central caries. It was done under local anaesthetic and I decided to get him off when the boat came, leaving me short. He was due for a change soon. On return he was keen to explain that the Uist dentist said the tooth had a crooked root.

The boat arrived later than expected because they had to reduce speed going around Barra Head. At 18.30 hours she was visible as a sparkling speck and at 19.45 hours she came in and stuck 20 yards off shore, so she drew off a little and wiggled on a few yards further. We climbed on the D8 and backed into four foot of water towards the ramp with water showering up through every hole in the floor. To my surprise we did it and I went off to examine a chap with flu. The Chiefy had met my uncle on their return to Stranraer (he was on holiday) and Joe

Gamgee sent me his best wishes. Back on 4074 again. We got one trailer off with the meat and mail and nearly got flooded in the back, so we decided to pull off and try again next morning at 07.00 hours after a high tide at 04.30 hours. We had tea in the Mess with Major Macgregor after I had roughly opened my mail and answered all the very important stuff.

September 23

Tony was first up. The boat, 4074, was up on the beach but was not going to be unloaded until 09.15 hours. We had been sent a 20ft boat out, larger than we needed, and therefore difficult to make secure.

Tony and I had both been up until 02.00 hours writing letters and he had less sleep than me. I took Peter Jones, the No. 1 on the LCT around the village, and then he took me back to the boat to show me some photos of me being transported to the trawler on the way over.

We watched them struggling with our 20 footer (it took them 2 hours to unload it) and soon there were four hefty fellows rowing it around to our slipway. The wind was getting up from the SE but we briefly took the visiting officers up to the Marconi, and they were impressed with the cold the hills and the bends. The boat had pulled off and they had a wet trip back on the dory. Apparently when they had pulled off the beach, they were almost driven broadside onto it. At 15.00 hours they plunged their way out of the bay with spray billowing over the bow.

September 24

I have marvelled in the wind on Skokholm, feared it at St Anne's Head, cursed it in the hunting field, and frozen in its icy blast on Cairngorm: however never have I experienced such blasts of wind as we had today. It blew up last night from the SE and by the morning was westerly, thus in the bay facing SE we were sheltered from the worst as it beat up on the other side of Dun, showering spray up 300ft, its unspent wrath rushing white past the end of the bay or using Dun gap as an acoustic accessory. We were spared the continuous strength, and the squalls coming down from the top doubled the usual maxima. The gusts tore at the waves breaking on the beach, sweeping whirling clouds of spray into the bay, each cloud making a rushing noise across the water and close to a hundred feet into the air. As the morning went on trawlers started coming in until there were eight present, one from Fleetwood and two Spanish. I spent most of the day inside watching the walls of the hut bending in, and listening to dustbins being blown around outside. A wooden door that had been flat on the ground took off and landed four yards away, and later a neat pile of three took off one by one as I was watching them quiver. At the signals hut a duckboard got blown onto the roof, and it was here that we were told the astonishing news that the LCT had not yet passed Barra Head (usually an eight hour journey) and was going to head straight for Loch Boisdale. A half full 40 gallon oil drum was rolling around the camp, having been blown from the upright position, and it is not surprising that the Enagyp gauge has gone. Do I write it off as 'lost during use' or 'gone with the wind'? After tea we dragged the dory further up the slipway and it was while resting from this, in sou'wester and oilskins that a tremendous gust blew in and I had to lie down.

After lunch the news had come through that the LCT could make no headway and was therefore abandoning all attempts to reach Loch Boisdale. Her small foremast had been blown away. Poor people.

September 25

I awoke to find most of the ships still in the bay, but the storm had abated somewhat. The Factor's House had shaken during the night.

September 25 (cont.)

The last trawler left at 22.30 hours. After tea I had walked up to Am Blaid to get a glimpse of any ships or damage.

September 26

A post breakfast Mist net produced more Meadow Pipits and one was a bird ringed last week before the storm, so it must have found shelter. A walk later showed none other than these around here. We heard on the RT that LCT 4074 had decided to head for Cainryan and arrived there at 10.15 hours having a naval vessel standing by and a lifeboat warned. Journey time c. 64 hours.

September 27

A mouse has learnt to open the Longworth live traps to look for perks when the trap is not set and is closed. I am now marking them to get some idea of their movements. Morning wind was E f. 5 but was veering to SE. On my return was told that the boat had left Cairnryan at16.00 hours and ETA tomorrow would be 15.00 hours expecting to beach at 22.00 hours. This would mean an all night loading and working on Monday as she was staying over two tides. During the evening we had another film, this being the third since the projector arrived last week. The wind rose later.

September 28

Sunday. The OC went to bed at 00.30 and had a final worry about the 20ft boat which we had reluctantly accepted off the LCT. It was too big and heavy and they had not sent a low loader. It had been tied to the buoy, which itself was anchored and attached by a wire hawser to the pier. Q. Birch REME put his head around Tony's bedroom door before we had risen, 'Sir, I have some bad news'. Tony said, 'I know, the boat's gone'. Well it had. He who had overruled our choice had forgotten to overrule the sea. Examination showed that a metal junction had broken and the boat was only attached by its own 'pulling in and out rope'. One side was missing but the engine still there. The sea was still heavy and the wind now a gale. The first patient of the day was a young Gannet which had been found on the shore and brought in in a large white bag. Young Gannets are brown and do not become quite white until they are five years old, spending much of their younger years off the coast of NW Africa. They have spent weeks using their large pointed beak to fence with their neighbours and this has to be avoided. Observation during the night after it had selectively preened each long feather showed that it did so with eyes closed, and when sleep came it was taken not only with its beak and face between its wings on its back, but also with its secondary wing feathers arched over like a fan to cover its crown. An hour or so spent with maps and a walk to the signals unit and the evening finished with a prolonged drinking session at the bar which as MO I was now theoretically in charge of.

September 29

The SE wind had abated and left us with occasional heavy showers sweeping across a calmer sea. After breakfast I did my rounds of the mouse traps, marking those mice who were not marked. The only in patient was the Gannet who assumed its photographic air once taken out of a sheet and placed on the shore rocks. Later it was seen wandering down to the sea, having a drink and swimming off. I was given a lift up to the Marconi and did my thrice weekly seal count in Glen Bay. Looking across to the Stacs I could see that there were more brown juveniles than white adults on the cliffs. I had done letters in the morning and more after tea, interspersed with more blood samples.

September 30

The boat got in at 05.30 hours but was not going to be able to stay over two tides because regulations stated that all craft will be clear of the island by September 30. This is an eminently sensible decision because of the higher incidence of severe gales, and the seasonal presence of the sandy ridge 30 or so yards out from low tide level, replacing the sandy beach. But it should have been a tapered boundary and reminds me of the twice yearly appearance on Unit standing orders such as 'June 10. Winter will begin on Sept 15'.

At 10.00 hours with a fair swell, and the sea still tearing through the holes in the ramp it went to the end of the bay, turned around and started its run in onto the beach. High enough but too far to the left. He opened his doors, and on deciding to try again, found he had difficulty in getting off. Q. Birch then took the D8 down and gave her a shove, certainly getting her off but not helping the door much. Once off he then took another rush and stuck on the sand ridge, however then he discovered that he could not get her doors open and had to withdraw into the bay again. While all this had been going on their dory landed and left the mail, a Major from the War Office, a Major from Scottish Command and an RAOC Captain from Carlisle. Each one later sought me out to impress me, each in their own way. Judgements were made but kept to ourselves. They all had their own 'egos' to smooth. How were they to deal with the fact that the craft had for the moment given up trying to beach. It was raining hard and agitation was appearing. They peered out of the window and sought comforting words from us; the only one to come was an announcement from Tony Riach that one of them had been appointed to be the President of the Court of Enquiry into the loss of the boat. One of those on the Board was the man who had bungled the choice and delivery. After lunch they settled down to consider the evidence and while the three wise men deliberated, the boat crept off round the corner and no one knew why or where, or when it was to return. Anyhow it eventually did so at 17.00 hours and we learnt that we were to have to ferry all we wanted the 600 yards from the vessel. This was to be the last supplies for six or seven months other than a three weekly mail bag via Fleetwood on a trawler on its way to the Icelandic fishing grounds.

Q. Birch and two others went on board in the first trip. After the crew of the dory returned, two people and the No. 1 had got it into the quay with great difficulty owing to the swell and the rising tide. Once on board they had started ripping open the packing cases to sift out the essential goods. A crowd of us were waiting on the quay under the impression that only a few journeys could be managed, were a little surprised when the first load consisted of Rinso and Tide, the second of 16fl oz tins of Guinness, the third a repeat of the second, and the fourth Pale Ale. Soon a regular routine set in. Tins of Guinness were being thrown out of the boat to a row of slip fielders on the quay who passed them back to soldiers behind. The dory would come to about 10 yards of the quay using her motor, about turn, and then come in with oars and the swell in reverse. Out would come the stern rope which I would grab and run with along to the far end of the quay to hold taut with one other person. Then would come the bow rope thrown to someone standing behind me while I was catching the stern one, and Corporal Pare who was standing knee deep on some steps grabbing the boat amidships, doing his best to keep it off the quay but not too far off. Tension had to be fairly constant to prevent the prop fouling a hawser astern. Corporal Pare was being held in his precarious position by a rope around his waist tied to our water loving Bombardier Harris. Intermingled with these human stanchions were a number of 'cricketers' catching cans of booze made slimy by spilt washing powder. Each time the boat left the quay we manhandled what we had to the one toner which had been backed down the slipway and stood with rear wheels in the sea. There was just enough time to get formed up for the next trip: more beer, more Guinness, and occasionally sacks of fruit, boxes of tools and sacks of potatoes.

One by one the officers left, the most impressive exit being that of a tall rotund figure who put one leg right in the water, crawled to the bow and hung on for love of life which he must have thought was about to slip beneath the waves. The darkness arrived and the lights of the ship came on. The orange floodlight we had fixed up proved a great help because the moon had not yet shown from behind the hill.

We all had hurried supper but what did that matter when so much essential equipment and stores were with us. The new tractor would have to be left on board with some furniture, and when Q. Birch came ashore he told us that tins of beer were rolling around the deck. In the last but one boat Tony Riach left us; a man for whom we all had great respect and was cheered off the island with hurrahs and the refrain of, 'for he's a jolly good fellow'. He waved and took off his hat. Tony had been brought out of semi-retirement, with no possibility or wish for promotion, and therefore having no need to be 'nice' when anger was needed in an upward direction.

The RA were jealous of their command position but it was awkward that the Unit on Hirta had more technical supporters than Gunner combatants; but they were needed and most of the REME Guided Weapon Specialists, having been on courses with Decca etc were singled out for the firm to buy them out and make them well paid civilians who they sometimes hired back to the War Office.

I never had an ill word with Tony. He may have slightly resented a junior officer having ecological control at certain times, and he did believe in silence at breakfast. He reluctantly allowed the morning shipping forecast. I used its barometric readings to allow me to draw a map of the weather systems. George Langford RA the new OC went on a quick trip to the craft to sign for the change of boat and then bought it back with two of the Crafts Crew and Q Birch. The two crew took the second dory back. Ten of us pulled the new boat up the slipway easily.

All this activity had taken place close to the medical centre. At 09.45 hours the main brace was spliced by Private Rhodes and myself (we had the medicinal rum in the drug cupboard). At 22.15 hours we walked outside to see a large friendly but sad moon peeping around the edge of Oiseval. The sky was clear and a few streaks of the aurora stabbed up around Conachair behind us to the north.

At 22.45 hours the ship swung and started moving, and with ex Ack Ack Sgt. Tombes at my side, and hunting horn at my lips, I blew her 'away' and blew her 'going home'. Sailing out into the sea: she left us for the winter.

Chapter Three

....

Gannet Sitting

The Autumn

Most of the several islands I have stayed on have a routine centred around 'The Boat'. It is not a God; but a means of aiding one's self help: and even God demands self help.

When the last craft had gone we were left to our own resources to manage, for there was no more maritime connection for six months other than the Fleetwood trawler Margaret Wick *which would be calling every three weeks on its way out to the Icelandic grounds, and a converted deep sea trawler called the* Mull. *Our Signallers were able to contact the Unit at Benbecula by RT for sending written messages by morse code or by voice, and the latter were often used for informal chat.*

The trawlers always preferred not to get too close to the quay and sometimes did not even hove to. We needed to get a party of ten to get the boat down and up, and three untrained crew would join the only skilled soldier seaman to cross over to the boat to get the Royal Mail. The trawler crew were co-operative and sympathetic but the Mull *crew were unskilled, disobedient, and scared; the only time they were content was when they were in the sanctity of Lochboisdale harbour.*

Because the last craft had not been able to beach properly we did not have all the material resources we had asked for; but we would manage. That is how the soldiers felt, and all the specialist electricians, plumber, 'chippy', cooks, and the officers would help out if asked. Some were going to be here until the Mull *emerged, and others until mid March. Corporal Pare was a versatile soldier but it was not that that kept him until March. It was the fact that he had the same blood group and Rhesus type as the MO, and both of us needed each other.*

The boat we had asked for had not been sent, and when I had asked for Cold Wet Boots for the lads on safety grounds, I was told that as St Kitts was in the West Indies the indent was turned down. A request for a heavy object was granted but would we notify the authorities of our nearest railway station? This upset us but no autumnal depression showed. We became familiar with the jobs of others, and I took on some less military ones. These included being Camp barber, Catering Officer, Met. Officer, and in charge of the bar. None of these came into my medical education but I did have sharp scissors. The styles were variable and when one soldier was asked when on leave who had last cut his hair and said his doctor had, there was a cool reception to his military humour. The bar work was efficiently done by my medical Sergeant with thoroughness and tact and I was soon sending off thrice daily climatic reports to Benbecula airport using Aero Code. At a sea post one got clear and sharp frontal conditions before they were muddled by coastline and hills. A thunderstorm in December and a change in the speed of a front both altered the midday weather forecast.

As Catering Officer I attended the drawing of rations for the week on every Saturday morning where I learnt a lot from the qualified baker from North Wales, Ifor Cunnah and an excellent chef from South Boisdale, George Maclellan.

October 1

While walking up top by the Marconi Radar building I walked up a flock of 34 Snow Buntings and there were also just over into Glen Mor several Lapland Buntings feeding singly. I surveyed some drains in the afternoon and did some digging later on.

October 2

During the morning I initiated the digging of a pit for the residue of the cesspit and took the plumber around the field explaining the attributes and faults of the drainage system. During the afternoon I sorted out the surgical instruments, placing them in the new shelves provided in the drug cupboard, and then set off for the Gap so as to turn left up onto Conachair via the cliff edge, pausing on the way to regain my breath and listen to the Fulmars wheeling around the cliffs. There are many thousands here and perhaps in these high pressure conditions they have come from afar prospecting for a ledge for next year. To the east Boreray gently smoked like a volcano, and from the top of Conachair, the actual summit being 90ft higher than my cliff path, and the cliff drop of 1300ft to my right, this was a magnificent sight but left that anatomically unexplainable discomfort in the pit of the abdomen. The second highest is on Soay where the sheep originally came from, and the third is the Kame of Foula off Shetland.

On my return I walked towards Mullach Mor collecting 350 yards of loose telephone wire on the way. The hot sun had given way to a deceitful heavy shower so I ran most of the way back to camp (*I was still in shirt sleeve order most of the time*), getting back at 17.00 hours. As I could not get any wetter I bathed before supper, had a film after, and spent time writing up bird notes with an ear tuned to Tchaikovsky's 5th Symphony. Bed after midnight.

My bedroom is in the roof space of the Factor's House and has a door to a small landing outside which is common to the gable end room opposite. There is ample room and a good light and a roof window 1ft 6" x 2ft 4" through which I can lie in bed and watch the weather. A few days ago a letter arrived telling me that I was to measure my bedroom windows for curtains. Politely I replied that the window was too small in that even pulled to one side they would exclude the light, and if as long as had been suggested, would hang onto the bed and prevent me getting into it. A letter was sent back to me insisting that Regulations insisted on them. I never heard any more.

October 3

No sooner had I sat down at my desk than Private Rhodes said he had asked to go and help on top. I accepted the lift. It had been raining but I need not have doubted that the sun would appear for it was fine until 17.00 hours with very little wind. Having done a round of the top I joined them in the Radar and helped them work out the echoes they were getting. Boreray was easy to see and to the NW were two fishing vessels close together. Over the top of Boreray were the Flannans, about 60 miles away and NE of us Lewis could be seen.

Over the top of the Long Island one or two peaks on Skye could be made out. The first Redwings were seen and the Lapland Buntings are getting tamer. I walked down for lunch and in the afternoon worked on the pool at Tobar Childa (*the Well of the Well*) opening up a sphagnum bog, served in the bar at night, washed my sheets, tucked into my polar down sleeping bag and started reading Winston Churchill's 'History of the English Speaking People'.

October 4

If such a day never occurred again I should not be surprised. It was a day of several surprises and experiences. The lad with urethritis duly reported sick and I took samples and stained them eventually using the 1/12" object glass to interpret it. Then I went to supervise the clearing of the cesspit following on my work a few days ago. We were not able to empty the middle liquefaction tank and the plumber told us that a bolt had worked loose and the landside tank had a faulty valve. Therefore both were emptied under the sea much to the joy of the gulls and only the seaside one was to be allowed to fill again.

While we were doing this smelly job the two Spanish trawlers came into the bay from around Dun and anchored close onto the buoy. The OC decided to get the boat out and a party of four non Spanish speaking soldiers armed with four loaves of bread boarded the two vessels, which were now tied together. When we got down our boat had returned with a large amount of fish which they had exchanged for the bread. There had been no mention of Gibraltar and this all needed immediate attention and under the careful guidance of Cpl. Pare (the chap with my blood kinship) who appeared to have done this job before, I removed heads and guts and filleted and then skinned for about 2 hours. Several of the hake were very large and had herrings as much as 6" long bent up double inside their stomachs. There were also haddock which were prepared for breakfast tomorrow, and the hake was filleted for the deep freeze. By 18.30 hours I had two indications for a bath, the fishy smell and the effects of the cesspit. My line of thought was disturbed by a hooting in the bay, and a stout trawler coming round Dun into the bay, semaphoring us. It was the *Margaret Wicks*, our Fleetwood mail boat and within two minutes a roar went up from our shore when they realised what it was. I hurriedly got a letter written when our boat went out for the second time today, but it seems that most of it was official mail.

I then took four people out to the Spanish trawlers with lemonade bottles and three pieces of rather old stewing beef, which we climbed on board with to present. They filled our bottles with wine and we took lessons in catching mackerel and getting the wine into our mouths from a leather bottle by squirting it.

Once back the wine was doled out and soon after a basket of silver hake arrived from the trawler. This was fine fish and was duly filleted while the mackerel were cooked and eaten with toast and butter.

An eventful day, and although material gains were of least importance, it is worth recording that for four large loaves of bread, half a tin of tobacco and some stewing beef, we obtained 80 x 14" haddock, 25 x 18" to 24" hake, 30 x 20" silver hake, 12 x 14" mackerel, 10 pints of red wine.

October 5

Fish for breakfast; excellent. Afterwards read a Sunday paper which was two weeks old and started on yesterday's log.

Generally a quiet day with some wind, some showers, and enough sun to collect lying behind a cleit.

October 6

A post tea walk produced two Water Rail where I had been digging at Tobar Childa.

October 7

A fine day with great clarity of vision. From the top, which I reached in summer dress and sweat on my brow, I looked down the full length of the Outer Hebrides, probably over a hundred degree arc, from the edge of Lewis to Barra Head. Included in this were the tops of the Barra peaks seemingly being islands, and white seas breaking on the Monachs further north, and the Flannans with a bright white lighthouse almost hidden by Boreray. Back through my favourite spots. After lunch I filled a large cavity in someone's molar tooth. A walk around Oiseval this evening, from where I make my counts of seals on Dun.

October 8

There have now been four or five chances to peep at Radar sets while birds were flying and feeding, or returning from feeding. Certain sea-birds leave a distinct pattern in their route or mode of flying. Gannets returning having fed some distance away will come in small groups in a straight line but often not line ahead. Many seem to come straight from Barra Head, as if going around it from the Minch, and in all the time I have watched in the South end of the Long Island, I have never seen birds crossing the land. They probably also come through the

Sound of Harris. Evening sorties into village bay could be birds just relieved off the nest or birds who have just finished a long trip and are filling in time.

Yesterday's flock of 800 to 1000 feeding off Soay were a fine spectacle probably concentrating around a large shoal of fish, for birds were falling and sitting on the water so densely that they needed to hover above to find a place to dive into. At one time it resembled a Broadway ticker tape parade as they fell into the water at 8–10 per second.

October 9

Indoor work followed by a windy walk PM when at times it was difficult to hold the glasses steady. When I arrived back the first boat load of an eventual party of eight or nine Spaniards had landed and were having tea and cakes. The vino arrived with the second load, by which time a darts and a billiards match were going. For the latter it seemed that the international language of grunts and groans suffices, but darts explained in a Glaswegian accent was more difficult.

The sea must have been calm because some one had rowed the book back alone, so I called him up with my hunting horn and he took 15 minutes to get alongside the quay in the swell. The Spaniards seemed to cover all 'morphs' of our society as did Snow White and the Seven Dwarfs, but it all helps.

October 10

More writing this morning and then filled two front teeth of a generator attendant. Head butting is common in Glasgow. There are three attendants who do eight hour shifts day and night and every one of us has a tutored session. There are now c. 200 Grey Seals on Dun and a bull of great size has 'opted out' for a rest by our quay. I authorised the use of a Nature Conservancy line and five of us went out and caught mackerel with the Coxswain in charge.

October 11

Mackerel for breakfast and I felt full all morning. A lone trawler I saw far out to sea turned out to be our mail boat. I was now *ipso facto* the Postmaster and was getting mail from far sources seeking my stamp. Post Office, St Kilda, North Atlantic seems to reach us. Letters today from Morton, Dr Lack and others.

October 12

Sunday. A few Geese and six Whooper Swans had arrived in what was probably a cyclonic movement from Iceland. Film tonight.

October 13

Stocktaking in the Canteen this morning. Filled three more teeth this afternoon. My popularity as a dentist is because no drilling is involved. For a few days now the Sheep have been very hypergonadistic; the tups are still in 'clubs' but a 'Top Tup' has been seen in a chase after a ewe in oestrus. My mouse trapping and marking continues. The days are less rushed but a climb is done most days even though they are still less productive on top.

October 14

The Geese are Pink feet. Redwings of the Icelandic race now in the village and a walk halfway up today confirmed the NW wind that had brought them. More tooth filling today. Film at night.

October 15

Another hour's dental work this morning. Wind still NW and glimpses of sun flashed onto the vegetation between sharp showers; a vegetation which with its yellow hue had a more autumnal tint than two weeks ago. A walk around some of the boundary wall of Gleann Mor showed that Glen Bay was getting some shelter in this wind from the Isle of Soay, but even being a mile from its water the squalls blowing onto it caused airborne spray to salt over my binoculars. Getting back to the Decca set I could see seven Spanish trawlers in.

October 16

The wind was still blowing from the NW, f. 5. When a westerly wind has an element of north in it the bay becomes calm. After lunch I got a lift up to Am Blaid, picking up one of the ACC cooks on the way. We walked up the road to Marconi for a while venturing on to the vegetation off the road, but it was not to be for long as here the wind took away your breath off your lips and blew the tears from eyes to ears. Talking was impossible and it must have been 50 to 60 knots. We took advantage of this and went down the west side of Mullach Mor into the head of the Gleann, leaning into the wind, heading for Gob-na-h airde (*Point of height*), the eastern point of the bay. Here we lay down and jammed ourselves into a cleft safely peering out to sea, but not safe from spray even at 150ft. I got splashed regularly but soon realised that one had to turn over seven seconds after you heard the bang of sea on rocks below with the clear cloudless blue sky above. We could see the waves breaking on the Boreray Stacs 120 to 170ft into the air. Half an hour's puff and we were again on Am Blaid, and down in time for tea. The Spaniards had

48

anticipated the wind would drop and started to leave, again leaving victuals behind.

October 17

Soon after 09.00 hours I started stock taking again in the Canteen. I was not able to take advantage of the glorious sunshine until after lunch, when I got a lift up to Marconi on Mullach Mor. There was not even a breeze as I sat and looked over an almost innocent serene Glen Bay, with a large flock of Snow Buntings flying against a blue sky.

Hardly more than 20 adult Gannets visible on the Stacs, but I think I can see some brown young. My route up to Conachair (hero of a legendary Irish tribe of terrific strength), where I could marvel at the thousands of Fulmars wheeling in the air and along the cliff edge. A diagonal path down the Village face took me to Tobar Childa in time for tea.

October 18

Stores in the morning, a mirky wet day, a book by Robert Henriques, and made a start on a plasticine model of the island, showing as may of the paths that are walkable in detail.

October 19

Sunday. The morning was spent as I intend to spend all Sunday mornings: home for the day, the Archers, Music Magazine, Concert Choice, etc. but big ideas were disturbed by a message to say that the *Mull* intended to come in at 1800 hours. At 1300 hours, after the news, there was a programme on the autumn migration from Peter Davis in Fair Isle, Dr Ennion at Monkhouse, Bert Axell from Dungeness, someone from the Scillies and Kate Barham from Skokholm. I only knew Peter well, but had been at sites close to the others. I found the wind strong at top. I returned again over the south face of Conachair.

The *Mull* came in at 18.00 hours but could not get the passengers off until 20.00 hours. The wind is still NW so Col. Cooper and Major Mac ate with us and stayed the night.

October 20

The wind slowly dropped over the morning and most of the time was spent talking to Mac about island matters. Later I went across to the *Mull* in one of the empty boats that had brought boxes from the boat. I saw the Captain and discovered that he intended to send across 400 yards of cable and did not seem in mind to do it in a way that would suit us. I insisted it was coiled properly into the boats so we could unload it with more ease, rather than having to lift the tight coiled wire. This was duly done, so we spliced the mainbrace in the Mess before lunch. It started to drizzle. Tea then a bath, did some reading and then served behind the bar.

October 21

I spent some time in trying to get Cowglen Lab to change their chlorine figure sent to us: they twice maintained it was 15 ppm, but at that level it was swimming bath strength, so I wrote to the DDMS to get his help. They were probably out by a factor of x10. They started laying the cable with the lurching and tossing D8. Film at night.

October 22

A difficult diagnostic problem with the neck of a Storm Petrel before breakfast. It was allowed half an hour's rest, and self the same time for breakfast. It appeared to have an injury to its neck going into its oesophagus or was it a foreign body coming out of its 'food pipe', or was it a piece of 'voice box'? Some necrotic material was removed and was healed over by evening so I released it. It gave a thankful call of relief as it flew off, so at least its larynx was intact. A WT message arrived to tell me that the chlorine concentration had been .15 ppm and not 15 ppm. In the presence of good health as there is now we will leave it as it is, with a very minor alteration upwards.

Cloud down to 600ft today.

October 23

Morning at work and after lunch clambered up the gully to Mullach Sgar (*summit cleft*) using the cable to help. Eventually walked down to the Dun gap where I reprimanded two gunners who were throwing stones at a seal, as I had also to do this morning when two were manhandling a young seal.

October 24

An unhappy day for the two Geese whose physical frailty fell to human's mental frailty. Once the crime had been suspected and then detected I handed the case over to the OC.

October 25

Morning work in the MI room and went around the camp with the OC and RSM, and before lunch the former gave the men a pep talk about grumbling. Westerly wind and very misty up top, so I kept to the village where I put up a Willow Warbler. During the evening I served behind the bar and resisted all temptation to be baited into talking about Geese.

October 26

Sunday. I listened to my Sunday programmes until noon. I then saw the first record for the island of a Black Redstart, followed by a first winter male Blackbird, a Song Thrush, and Fieldfare. Do birds think of 'salvation' when in low cloud fifty miles from the last land, they see us without the guiding light of a lighthouse?

During the evening we had a long prearranged film 'The Goose Steps Out'. Tomorrow the OC deals with the Goose Killers.

October 27

While we were doing the stock taking the criminals presented themselves with an abject apology. How long this remains in their minds remains to be seen. Otherwise a quiet day in the village and I dealt with the soldier who had had abdominal pain in the morning and been admitted, by promising to deal with his worries tomorrow when anyhow he would feel better.

October 28

Yesterday's patient discharged. More dental work after tea. Film during the evening. The night I emerged into after it was so 'intoxicating' with a bright moon, feeding sheep, a warm breeze and a glistening bay that I went a walk and was loath to climb into bed.

October 29

Half cloud cover or less and the bright sun which shone onto hills, now rather yellow, was determined to display the fading year. The grass growth has slowed and there are more sheep in the village area where the level of nutrition is higher. Some sheep browse the Fescues on top of the cleits but still there are nuptial chases. One visit up top today between coffee and lunch, and a walk in the village later. During the late evening I propped up the bar from the serving side.

October 30

Blood letting first. 30 or 40 Redwings in the village in a compact flock and not just wandering around feeling lost. After tea I read and after supper did bar duty again.

October 31

Stock taking morning in the Canteen and soon after someone came down from the top to say that a tup had got entangled in telephone wires by the Decca. However it was not airborne so to write 'lines' would be less alarming. I walked to the quarry and then got a lift. The job was half done when it broke away like a triumphant scrum half and ran as if it was dragging a wing forward with it. Lunch over, we then prepared for the *Margaret Wick* with the mail. On my village walk I saw Redwings come into the village from over the Gap, spread across the village and creeping across the ground leading up to the quarry. Later I heard many leaving, flying out to sea over the Factor's House. The trawler came in at 22.30 hours and we made two trips to her. On the last one I went with some blood samples which were to be put on ice somewhere for two weeks before being dispatched from Fleetwood.

Chapter Four

....

Fulmar

November – the Year's Low

Once the year had turned I looked back at this month with some gloom, for so much was trailing off and so much around the corner but not in sight. Yet we had to keep on our toes most of the time, and one does this best from an even keel. When letters did arrive in a trawler I opened mine over 48 hours, because a response could await the end of the week or longer, and anyhow went fishing first. Films were shown more frequently, and I lived behind the bar for longer with the evenings shorter. Aero code weather reports went out thrice daily, and every two weeks I sent a bird report to Ken Williamson at the BTO at Oxford in code. This had to be so done from when our OC was told by the OC in Benbecula that Gunner X wanted leave in January for his girlfriend Mary's birthday party. X had persuaded a mate signaller to send it in clear, it had been picked up by a Polish trawler, leaked to our own spying system, and sent to us as an example of sloppy communication.

I was one up on all of them. Some years later a cousin-in-law told me that on a recent social occasion he had been approached by someone who had discovered that his wife's maiden name was the same as 'that chap on St Kilda'. He then said that at a social 'intra' embassy Moscow function four years previously a Russian had in a relaxed state asked him who the St Kilda Source was for it was one of the few codes from the G W unit that was still unbroken. Simply it was based on the number of the bird on the British Ornithologist Union's list, a straight number for the number seen, and a six figure number for the date. They got their answer at the next Christmas Party!

I was not too often gloomy, for the senior tup in the village flock was sowing his seed well after persuasive nuptials, and there are fluctuant numbers of Fulmars around the most dense nesting places, seemingly collecting from a distance and stimulated by a common factor, all planning for the next breeding season.

The dominant tup examines each ewe he claims while the younger tups watch on. The dominancy is sorted out during the grazing months amongst the tup clubs; rarely by fighting but often as eye glancing by deliberately moving closer to the head of another tup, who then moves on. The chase itself has the most dominant male behind the ewe, who is often accompanied by this year's bewildered lamb at heel. Other males then follow in an irregular line. This is so time demanding that the dominant tup has to rely on fat reserves built up during the summer, and when it is all over, the ewes are left on the better pasture and the tups reassemble in clubs in less favoured areas, losing their hormonal drive and more likely to die during the winter (this could be an advantage as it reduces the problem of in breeding the next year).

November is the time for preparation for the spring. Jobs were being done which would not be allowed to clash with preparations for firing next year. At the same time as I was creating a model of Hirta from plasticine, I was walking at least the village area every day. Last mail my authority arrived from the NTS enabling me to act for them, so these walks were reportable to Charlotte Square.

November 4

The Snow Buntings up top were split into two flocks. A PM done on a Red Breasted Merganser showed liver infection and peritonitis, and two large tapeworms in the lower gut.

November 5

Probable Common Seal calf born in front of Manse.

November 6

Repairs to putty around an MI room window. Lads finished the library shelves in the MI room and I wrote out Library Rules. Sheep count in the village.

November 7

I led a small voluntary repair and cleaning party in the church. Non denominational Remembrance Day Service Sunday but paucity of furnishings would suit a Wee Freeze Service.

November 8

Another 'go' at church.

November 9

A day of Remembrance of a subject that concerned us all. We held a small service I organised in the church, all in best uniforms except one rather bolshy Sgt. who came in civvy clothes. Two soldiers came out of their huts in sloppy clothes, saw the OC and myself smart, and ran back to smarten up. Onward Christian Soldiers, for those in peril on the sea, a lesson and prayer, and a 2 minute silence from the Cenotaph spoilt only by atmospheric noise.

A personal walk around Oiseval paths anti-clockwise to the Gap where Fulmars were displaying their aeronautical versatility, twitching the odd feather to re align without effort. Wind from the North. Read some more Lorna Doone then went for supper.

The *Boston Monarch* came in at 20.30 hours and we took off the mail, finding the landing a little difficult because the low tide had exposed some rocks below the pier, so after unloading we sent the boat back to the ship for safety to wait for the tide to rise, but still got very wet getting the boat up at midnight and a rum issue for those concerned after, with bread and soup. I was responsible for the rum but the cooks were ever alert, even when off duty, for this kind of need. Bed at 00.30.

November 10, 11, and 12

Very routine.

November 13

Wind free and warm. I put up a Woodcock while walking on the top. This is the time of the year that hundreds cross from Scandinavia to the northern Isles, if Fair Isle is typical.

November 14 and 15

Good conditions on top, enough to bring sweat out. D8 had done a few 'naughties' off the track.

November 16

Sunday. 'So early in the morning, just at the break of day.'

The high quality of the electricity between 07.45 hours and 08.30 hours was because I was doing an early turn of generator duty, having risen at 07.30 hours with a deep darkness over the island. All did 45 minute shifts today to give the attendants a day off. I had previously been advised of the safe limits on the gauge. My usual Sunday wireless listening. I confirmed the attendant's suggestion that the sheep slept up towards the Gap.

November 17

I did an anticlockwise tour of the village with mist covered heights above me, which went pink in the sunset. After tea I used the unit photographic equipment to develop a black and white film.

November 18

I started to audit the cellar accounts and the OC audited my canteen accounts. Voluntary advisable issue of vitamins started. Probably only C needed (*humans in common with guinea pigs cannot make their own, and the body stores only last 6 weeks*).

November 19

A blustery day. Wind S gale force. Ken Williamson's reply to my coded migration report to him arrived today by RT from Benbecula. My report had read:

> Last 255 Sept 1&4 stop last 380 ALBA ALBA Oct 21 stop. Oct 12 85&78 Brachi stop First 304 on Oct 03 under 12 until Oct 26 when MUSICUS MUSICUS arrived with 308 and 302 and 321, and 354 QUERY RACE stop. 300 of 304 on Oct 31 stop Letter follows stop.

His letter contained an account of many hundreds of migrants and Woodcock on November 2, 4, 5. What we had had was an overshoot from Fair Isle; but we did detect it.

November 20

Accounts all morning. Village in PM. After the evening film Cpl. Pare and self went up to the Decca Radar by lorry and I spent an hour varying the elevation and range to look for seabirds flying after dark, and there were none, so we did a quick check at Marconi and got back at 00.30 hours.

November 21

The audit continues and I feel like eating my meals in columns. In a hurry to get some exercise and got up to Mullach Sgar from the camp in 20 minutes (about 715ft up the road). A day of poor light.

······ *Chapter Four* ······

November 22

Boston Monarch arrived with much mail today. My glasses had their first day off since I arrived. During evening wrote to Graham Chance in Singapore with the Ghurkhas, he was a medic friend. A QARANC Lieut. Dorothy Savage had written to me ten days ago from Cowglen.

November 23

Sunday. In the village before lunch and up Ruaival after lunch. Used the gramophone during the afternoon. Warm S wind but forecast rain did not materialise.

November 24

Wind SW all day but moderate. Still much mail to do and missed break. Up to the Gap after lunch and back via village. Fulmars up in moderation.

November 25

It has been said of St Kilda that November is the quietest month of the year, with hardly a flicker of life to break the quiet monotony of the island. Perhaps activities have now settled down in that the vegetation no longer strives to keep pace with the sheep, and the mountain tops seem dormant in clouds, oblivious of the fact that below in the tiny camp, there is once again more activity than for twenty five years. Dare I write that we have had no storm for three or four weeks, or will the mountains once again throw back their winds down at us from their heights. Whatever the level of the island's winter torpidity, the Fulmars are awake, chattering, warning, head waving and observing possibilities with effortless gliding, on the ledges around the Gap and elsewhere. The poorly colonised areas are not used in this way, as if they lack the mutual stimulus of numbers.

Very little stirred on top and for the first time I noticed that the small parties of sheep had grazed the sward to the level the Soays and rabbits had on Skokholm, Pembrokeshire. Boreray looked silent but no doubt it was not without its tortuous winds amidst its crags. A film in the evening.

November 26

The boat was delayed and did not arrive in the bay until 16.00 hours. A wet foggy morning and fine later; the 'glass' was high enough to bring Fulmars to Dun. It was the *Mull* this time and it came with four Majors; Riach back again, Macgregor a revisit, Sutherland a Sapper (who I took a moonlight walk in the village after supper) and Maurice Francis who was attached to the Gunners. The lads did numerous trips ferrying equipment between *Mull* and quay, and did it with a good heart even though only one was a trained sailor. The *Mull* seafaring crew merely watched from the security of the rail.

November 27

It was originally intended that the boat would leave this morning, but the 'cream' of the Services' supply system were frightened of the tides in the Sound of Harris. However this allowed the visiting party to extend their activities, and they were to leave early tomorrow. Meanwhile the weather was improving and Fulmar numbers were increasing in the less favoured areas.

Michael Redgrave and Ann Todd in the film tonight.

November 28

The *Mull* was going to leave early and I rose from my sleeping bag at 5.30 hours, my sheets having been sent for a 'proper wash'. The moon was high over Mullach Sgar and a few sheep were browsing around the Signals Centre, a low level activity only occurring in good light. This diary is being written the morning after the events, so I have omitted reference to a lunar serenity.

A warning that trouble was impending came when in the half light I came onto the pier at 06.45 hours to see the dory and four occupants being swept by a huge wave like a surfboard around the right angle turn of the pier with four people struggling with two ropes to prevent the boat going onto the rocks. Immediately the boat was fulled back and we asked for the ship's boat, a 12 footer, to be sent out in two hours time, when the tide would be less full.

Under the affects of Avomine, most of the lads slept, but two hours later we were catching the ropes of the *Mull*'s boat as she slowly came into the quay. 'Mongaloid' Bob was watching from outside the *Mull* cabin and there was the usual scuffle and panic amongst the crew for this type of work was not akin to their liking in that most of their trips are done on selected days, free of wind, rain, and perhaps even waves. She works out of Cairnryan, dumping non used war materials.

The first lot of people and some luggage were put on and her engine drew her away from the pier and across to the *Mull*. The whole procedure of unloading and loading was always tricky, and in these conditions dangerous. It became even more so when during the second loading a huge wave stopped the engine and we needed all our strength on the stern ropes to stop her leaving the pier with the washed rocks a few feet away. Her gunwale top six inches on the port side of the stern was smashed, and every two minutes a larger wave would carry water into the boat which was not being allowed its natural rise and fall with the waves. Eventually they decided to row out of this dangerous situation with two to each oar, and reached the *Mull*.

From here they signalled that they were not coming back to us (too dangerous for his boat and crew) and we were to get our 'wee' dory out. With difficulty we took the remaining three people in this, rowing fast past the pier and then turning back to load off onto the boat. We got the last passengers back by taking it onto the pier rocks, getting them to jump out, and pulling the dory round the pier to the slipway, using its own ropes.

The *Mull* left at speed into the low sun, and we were again left.

November 29

No rain for several days. Short walk up top. 312 Seals on Dun.

November 30

Sunday. I got up at 09.00 hours with the sun well risen throwing a strong bright yellow light over the bay and village. The top summoned and Larry agreed. At least once a week he watches out for me. Larry was a bottle reared lamb handed over by the RAF.

Across the waters almost the full chain of the Hebrides could be seen slowly heaving themselves out of the water as I gained height. There are no ground feeding birds on top now, the Redwings only being in the village. It was warmish out of the north wind as I kept my eyes well ahead, walking towards the old wall circling around the west high end of the Glen, where it backs against the foundations of the Mullach Bi and Carn Mor cliffs, near the Lover's Stone, the testing area for those wanting a wife. Here I sat in the sun. Out of the local heft of 17 'Soays', 4 were pale, and 13 dark. 14 were female of which 7 were hornless.

During the time I was off in March '59 I went to Woburn and visited the retired shepherd of the 'flying Duchess' probably more noted for her support of migration work, especially on Fair Isle. We both sat in a dim room with a small fire, and we talked about her. He told me he did have pale lambs, and she accused him of allowing a farm ram in, threatening him with the sack. He denied getting a strange ram in, and subsequently killed and buried every pale lamb born.

The only noise was that of Rock Pipits providing the upper notes, and Fulmars the tenors. A silent Woodcock was put up on the way back. I returned with Larry at heel down the Gully and got back for lunch. A quiet afternoon and a film in the evening.

Chapter Five

....

Grey Seal Bull

Shorter and Longer Days

December 1

A dull misty day introduced by a glorious sunrise over the Long Island which outlined South Uist and others in a strong yellow and orange light. A mail boat expected in the afternoon so I could not leave camp, and anyhow had plenty to do outside there. My binocs never left their case. Boat came in evening after supper.

December 2

Today I put together a letter to James Fisher concerning Fulmar numbers with respect to time of year. I have brought his fine New Naturalist Volume with me and made notes from books by Sands, Martin, and Atkinson to give me a reasonably good brief, and a copy of Lonely Islands by Roland Svensson. Perhaps the latter is a favourite.

It was with this book that I had frightened the Quartermaster at Cowglen as to the type of landing he would need to make, but a few years later that my son and I had a wet two days on the Outer Skerries in the Shetlands, where Svensson had left his Island Drawings in the Village Hall.

December 3

At last we have got more Met. equipment. To celebrate we persuaded it to rain most of the day. My medics did most of the spade work with me.

December 4

More Met. work. One village walk.

December 5

Fewer Fulmars at Gap.

December 6

Such has been the paucity of birds that the appearance of a *Phyloscopus* (meaning 'leaf searcher') *collybita tristis* in a trench outside the Factor's House was a highlight.

I found it again in four wet areas in the morning and had good views so was able to suggest that its racial type was 'tristis' or Siberian. The use of the word 'suggest' was no longer needed after I saw this rather grey race of Chiff Chaff with a paler belly in Nepal many years later.

One Golden Plover seen. There is now an ACC Sergeant to supervise the Ration issue every Saturday, but I still have to be present and in charge, and it takes two hours to do.

December 7

Sunday. I have used every chance to listen to the test match at Brisbane, but no play today. Hail and rain this afternoon so I spent time modelling the paths in my plasticine.

December 8

As yesterday, with the addition of some waste pit digging.

December 9

Trawler on its way with the mail, and she only left Fleetwood yesterday with last Sunday's papers. She came in at 17.00. Film in evening.

December 10

After breakfast I went through my mail not as Postmaster, St Kilda, but as someone hungry for warm news from friends, and the warmth of colour. An old friend (Bep) had sent a 90+ year old lady (Cousin Clem) some flowers from me. Ken Williamson sent some reprints and an uncle and aunt (Peter and Marion) sent me some Christmas numbers of Punch and some coloured magazines.

I found myself looking many times at the red and the greens. We had neither here now other than some red paint still remaining on the oil drums.

December 11

A cold wind up top in the afternoon and we could see the snow covered peaks of the Uists where it had come from. There had been a wee influx of mainland birds with it: Redwings, a Lapwing, six Ravens, and a Blackbird. No Fulmars.

December 12

Rain most of day with strong wind.

December 13

The sea was swollen with stored energy this morning for the wind had abated during the night. It was warmer. A village street and Conachair base walk which produced my first Iceland Gull, an immature one.

December 14

Sunday. Dun Seal numbers about 360. No Fulmars. I listened to my usual Sunday programmes and found the Archers summary as my only connection with Birmingham.

December 15

I awoke to find our first Easterly gale and the Bay was quite a tumult, especially on the opposite side on Dun where fountains of white spray were being thrown into the air 300ft to 350ft high. Only two seals this side of the Island of Dun. A single lonely Barnacle and a great increase in Gulls, probably blown out of some mainland port. The signallers had no news of the boat, perhaps because their aerial had blown over, but somehow I doubt whether the *Mull* would attempt it even if every member of their crew were in triplicate. The wind started to back in the evening.

December 16

We hear that the mainland is getting a good dose of snow. Mullach Mor had a tinge of white on its top. The early part of the morning was spent coaxing the half built raft from the beach to the pier. The gale had tried to devour it even though it was built of two telegraph poles, a dozen duck boards and as many oil drums.

We put up the Stevenson Screen today. The *Mull* is still in the Minch. Probably wise.

December 17

It is now some time since I have been up top and and I wanted to look into Gleann Mor to see what it would be like to winter there if any group ever did. To get up top I had to wear a heavy weight Parka and goggles. There were patches of ice on the road towards the top and further along a sprinkling of snow on the grass. The glen was dim and dull, with only a few sheep to give any movements. The *Mull* was now at Loch Carnan and has decided to leave tomorrow. Shall we offer the crew a 'well earned break from work' and give them the site in the glen for a picnic?

December 18

As the day went on it became clear that we were not going to see the *Mull*, our relief boat, today, and probably not even tomorrow. The wind was cold and near gale force in the morning strengthening during (*to force 9 tomorrow*) late afternoon. I went up to the Gap where I got some shelter in relative warmth and without wind chill, but still shuddered with unruffled hair as the sea hit the cliffs about 400ft below.

December 19

Wind E, f. 9 greeted me on my walk to breakfast and it had got stronger by lunch time causing the sea to break 80ft to 100ft on Dun, and the 'sea water' came off the sea in the bay flying up high as a spray onto the village. Everywhere was wet, yet there was no rain until later in the day. Goggles were needed on my walk and a large 80 gallon oil drum, power driven by the gusts of wind, followed me up the road rather like a reluctant dog, more interested in the lampposts than an uphill walk. No masts, no lampposts, and a damaged Marconi Radar. In between the gusts the oil drum slowly travelled back the way it had come up, and then would poise ready to catch me up. I turned down towards Decca and looking over to Dun. The wind hit in strong jerks and were it not for my goggles progress would have been impossible as I could have not kept my eyes open. My face stung in the salt as if it was a gravel storm, and my binoculars, slung in their case on my back, struggled swinging around as if trying to get out.

The passage between Dun and Hirta was an inferno of water coming across the mouth of the bay, and the sea, streaked by the wind, threw up a deluge of spray, the residue of which hurt like hail a hundred yards from the cliff edge. In contrast the west side of the cliffs were immune from all but the gusts coming down them and smacking onto a resting sea.

Now for the return journey. A permanent Neanderthal crouch was safest and at times it was safest to be on one's knees, not in prayer or meditation, but just to allow the four points of contact needed in our ex ancestral 'tree'. The wind was not cold, but the long steady push with no break was wicked. Up here I could go straight, lean into the wind, hang my arms down, and my finger tips would be only nine inches off the ground. All steamer services over the Minch have been stopped.

December 20

Seas less. Larry (the lamb) took me a walk in the village.

December 21

Sunday. Awoke to find the wind had veered to the south, but there was still a swell. My sojourn with 'Music Magazine' was disturbed by the news that the *Boston Monarch* was due in the bay in ten minutes. Horror struck we roused the Sergeants and got the dory down. We got it away from the pier, however the wind or water was such that they were still a hundred yards away after ten minutes, and the trawler was still an uncomfortable half a mile off, unwilling to come any nearer. During a lull in the wind they made ground but soon lost it again. In wireless contact with the trawler we persuaded them to venture closer to the rowing lads (*none of them trained seamen*) partly by telling them there was a bottle of whisky there for them. Before the trawler reached them an oar broke and they were obliged to return. Revived by medicinal rum, and two fresh crew and oars, they set out again and after half an hour got there, the trawler immediately towing the boat further from the angry shores to safer waters. Having lowered the mail, the plunging trawler towed her 'baby' at heel nearer the pier, and cast her off. They had a wet landing but what did that matter when they were alive, and there was the Royal Mail safe. My letters are still unsent because the trawler will not get back to Fleetwood until after the New Year. She left us with multiple 'tooting'. A huge parcel arrived with Christmas fare from Dad and a few more will be left until Christmas Day before being opened. The Gunner who had asked me to remove most of a 'PAULINE' tattoo from his forearm (I then covered it with a 'split skin' graft from his upper arm) reports that it is well healed, and he seems so happy. I wonder what happiness there is in Pauline's household this Christmas.

December 22

'Sheep may safely graze' and apparently Whooper Swans also, for when looking into the North Glen from the top I saw four moving white figures moving in the Amazon's House: Ma and Pa and two youngsters, the latter a little dingy. I hastened back to tea, finding a Greylag on the way. The seals had returned to Dun. The camp workers had pulled the raft around to the slipway to repair it.

They were sure the *Mull* would leave for Hirta tomorrow and were sure the raft would make an easier approach to the *Mull* than a dory. They worked all night at it and had it tied to the buoy by dawn. This was quite a resurrection from when it looked like a dead butterfly, motionless, torn and with an occasional flick of its wing, flapping in the sea.

December 23

At 06.45 hours I was up and having breakfast with the moon shining on the hard outline of Dun across the Bay. At 08.00 hours with the wind SW, f. 2 the *Mull* came in 'all lit up'. With the raft as a floating pier the *Mull's* cutter was loaded with personal gear and those due to go off. I went on board to arrange a lying down place for my cook, George, who after

3 grains of intra muscular phenobarbitone for *hyperemesis maritinae* was now in a bed in the MI room.

The decorations that dad had sent on the trawler were now up in the MI room. The boat left at 11.30 hours and I spent some time putting fresh food away. Brief talk with Major Mac. Sorted mail.

December 24

Christmas Eve. The equinox has passed, the sun rises here at 09.15 hours and sets at 15.15 hours, giving us eight hours daylight, so much of yesterday's fun took place in the dark. I went over to the North Glen to see the Whoopers and by crawling on my belly in slight wetness was able to get to a spot seven yards from the four birds. A juvenile saw me first but as her soft note comment from her high neck got no response from the others who were grazing, she calmed down. I got back in time for the Festival of Nine Lessons and Carols from Kings College at 15.30 hours. We had a gramophone in the bar and I led the carol singing. There was much alcohol taken to make the inhibited vocalists feel more secure.

For many it was their first Christmas away from home. For me it was a working Christmas, or should I write 'on duty'. The last one had been on a winter warfare course in the Cairngorms, and the previous one emergency duty in hospital. But there were no nurses here for mutual and professional companionship.

December 25

Christmas day. At last bed at 01.30 hours. It may have taken seven people an hour to make the tea for the lads so that they could have it in bed at 8.45 hours with rum to follow, but it only took a loud hailer and a hunting horn to wake them.

Breakfast was so arranged that they could all have cold ham for breakfast, which in the view of the MO/Catering Officer is an essential requisite for a light breakfast: to allow room for lunch.

Before lunch we had the Sergeants in for drinks to prepare us for the customary job of serving Christmas to the lads, and washing up afterwards. The chicken was nice but when we sat down to it in our Mess it was cold. We finished feeling full in time to listen to the Queen. A small tea and light supper after which we had fun and games in the bar, which games I bore with good grace, and which most people seemed to enjoy.

December 26

Up at 9.00 hours. Wet and cloudy. About 10.00 hours I started laying a scavenger trail 'cum' treasure hunt trail. 20 lads left the MI room at 11.45. The majority were not fit enough to keep up with the leaders, but what with fizzing bottles of beer and half empty ale tins it was quite a sight and enjoyed by most of them. Even Larry the lamb was amongst the leaders at the final run in.

At 12.30 hours Tony Riach and I went for drinks at the Sergeants' Mess. Afterwards we partook of an excellent chicken, Christmas pud and Sauterne, all sufficient to make me fairly sleepy, and I retired to my room to Fulmar watch for an hour (*an expression originating when a birdy Doctor friend discovered that I was able to sea watch lying flat balancing my binoculars on my nose and eyes, and sleep*).

December 27

I climbed up to Mullach Sgar top (915 feet) via the Gully and did a quick walk of the village before doing so. The climb was damp from showers but I walked down to Ruaival on the maritime '*P maritima and coronopus* slope', a smooth short sward.

December 28

Sunday. I lay in bed until 09.00 hours listening to the rain and the wind blowing outside the Factor's House. Both were heavy at times but relaxed for my breakfast, as if it were a 'trying' child showing it could do a complete turn of the clock without permission; and then strike.

I did my washing this morning. In the afternoon it was fine to watch the westerly seas roaring past the entrance to the bay as a white line flashing in the thin sun. The Dun gap was a mass of leaping water from the seas beating up on the far side. Spray can be of two types here: the splash of waves off rocks, and the circling airborne shower sucked off the wave tops or even a flat sea, by the roaring winds coming down the mountain slopes and hitting the sea explosively, retreating upwards in a high spiralling trailing sheet to alight where it wishes (*most of our Na+ Cl– (Sodium Chloride) inland comes down in the rain*). Today boxes flew through the air and oil drums climbed the bank at the back of the beach as if it was a Normandy Landing.

Combined with the hail storms the noise was terrific. As the tide flowed, the swell increased, providing yet more water for the hungry heavens to grab. It flung itself across the pier and we were later obliged to pull the boat and the raft up the slipway and up to the Manse wall. The two Spanish trawlers came in for shelter, their twinkling lights in the bay gradually becoming less important as the moon came around Oiseval, lighting up the clouds of spray.

December 29

Dental and other minor surgery during the day.

December 30

A single Fulmar today. Two different gales in the last 24 hours.

December 31

Fulmars back at the Gap and Conachair hesitatingly, but a few on ledges.

1959

Soay Ewe Portrait

January 1

Today had a break in the continuous rain to allow it to snow. Soon all the ground above 400 feet was white except for the cleits where probably there was enough warmth from a little oven effect of the rotting faeces left by their nocturnal ovine occupants. Two films in the last week.

Analysis of the December Met. readings shows that on 16 days we had winds of strength force 8 or above. On no occasion in the last half of the month was the temperature at 09.00 hours below 40 degrees F or above 49.5 degrees F. 119.2 mm of rain in Dec. during 24 days.

January 2

Walks around the north glen and west cliffs.

January 3

Having issued some of the rations last night I finished earlier this morning. At 11.58 hours I was sitting by the window in the mess listening to the test match Summary. Tony and some others had gone up to the Rocket launcher near Mullach Sgar to fire some test rockets. None had been heard yet. Suddenly there was the expected swooooosh, and I immediately opened the window to see a twisted and angular smoke trail, and three or four seconds later heard a bang. The launcher was about a thousand yards from me, and I realised that something had gone wrong. My first thoughts were that someone up there was hurt, my second was that it would fall down here, and my third ridiculed both.

Little did I know that the bang was the rocket landing on the billets behind me – all six foot of a hundred pound body and a 35 pound concrete head; and going into the kitchen I walked out the back towards the billets not noticing the damage. By the time I had got back into the kitchen a very pale 'chippy' came rushing up to say that Corporal Williams had been hurt. A trail of blood led to my medical centre where a very pale 'Slim' was perched on a chair, blood dripping from his wrist. Apart from a small cut over the right eye, he had a swollen right elbow, a limp wrist, and a large cut on the back of it. Remedy: blankets, morphia, rest, shell dressing and assurance, and an hour later the wound was stitched, there being no fracture present.

Soon after the unexpected came through the roof Cpl. Haywood rushed to the signals centre to inform them up top. Apparently they hardly believed us, for although they realised it had gone astray, they imagined it had gone towards Boreray (it had been fired the opposite direction), but realising that we were being serious came rushing down dreading that human carnage had resulted. Fortunately this was not the case, but on examining it later it seemed that it must have travelled up 3000 feet plus before twisting down because it had lost a tail fin.

On hearing the noise those in the billet rushed to the window and a few seconds later it burst through the roof, embedding itself in a hole a foot deep in the concrete floor by 'Slim's' bed where he lay half sitting playing his guitar. There being plenty of room in the hut, the lads had arranged their 6 foot metal lockers in complicated patterns to provide some privacy. These withstood the concrete fragmentation, and the scattering of pieces of metal, plaster, wood and a few bricks from the six foot wide hole. They worked on the damage the rest of the day. The good Corporal when seen later was almost apologetic, 'I was only practicing a few chords Sir,' as if the heavens disapproved.

Oiseval produced a short thick snowstorm for me, so hood up, I went downhill the right direction. No Fulmars today but perhaps a few yesterday.

January 4

Sunday. It is now two weeks since we have had a trawler. I spent much of the day attending to water courses.

January 5

Snow around the Factor's House and on the hills. Fantastic views from the top of far and near, and there were still snow showers coming across the sea.

Ambient temperatures:

```
4ft shade                   35 degrees F
Ground                      31 degrees F
Ground in sun               38.5 degrees F
Water emerging from ground  48 degrees F
Water stagnant              37.5 degrees F
Water in stream 3 mins out  47.2 degrees F
```

January 6

The mouse trapping still continues; there are perks to go with it. Adequate hay bedding and a variety of food. One mouse found dead elsewhere. PM exam showed good body reserves of fat, plenty of food in gut, a large tapeworm and some nematode worms (*an exam later of the cestode said that the secondary host were a flea and sheep*).

In this snow any birds are feeding around the flushes from springs where the relatively warm water has turned the grass green, so I have widened them by blocking some exits of water from the flushes and have had lapwing, Starling, Redwing and Turnstone feeding there. A Turnstone re-trapped; ringed as a first winter bird in Sept 1957. All temperatures, bar the ground water, up on yesterday. Many of the Outer Hebridean islands now appear quite white with snow.

Ken Williamson has sent me an account of birds at Fair Isle. They see a hundred of X there and we get <10 here. We are a last resort for the lost.

January 7

Boston Brittania came in at 21.00 hours. She had left Fleetwood on December 26 and had difficulty in getting us on RT while she was secluding herself from the f. 11 gale, and then went fishing.

She had arrived at ebb tide and it was clear that 2 hours further flow was needed. The trawler reluctantly accepted this, and at 23.30 hours 20 of us assembled to get the 20ft cutter out from off the slipway.

An all corps group of us pushed and pulled, swam, waded and crawled over the rocks where she had grounded on her way out to move her further out. Mail and fish were collected, and with a rising tide the boat was brought back in with greater ease. Q. Birch was quite exhausted and needed medical attention, and the remaining bodies pulled the boat on to the bowser chassis we had improvised.

Unfortunately we could only get this half way around the corner and for the next hour we used a 'one toner' and hawser on the top of the low cliff to haul it round. Then the three toner was added to give a different line of pull. There were only six of us left at 03.30 hours, many having got very stressed. We had been working for four hours, the most dangerous time being the launching of the boat and the most difficult the retrieval. Medicinal rum and tea, and then bed.

January 8

Mail sort this AM and I wrote to Dad, and Dorothy Savage at Cowglen. A trawler arrived in the evening and we went through a smaller and safer repetition of last night, or rather early this morning. It took me an hour and a half to get through my mail. Wonderful.

January 9

Snow overnight. Activities today included blocking water drainage ditches to increase the size of warmer water flushes (T 46.6 F) for the feeding Starlings and Turnstones, going through my mail, finishing a letter to the Medical Graduates Newsletter (Birmingham), and starting my Swedish Linguaphone Course. I started on tomorrow's Ration issue.

January 10

Another fresh covering of snow. At 09.45 hours I resumed my work in the Ration Store, weighing out the powders. My proficiency increases, and at 11.00 hours it had been done. The variable problem is the allocation of Sardines/Pilchards. The sun on the gull area and village are dramatic and I went 100ft up Oiseval to photograph it (*it was this photograph that was used by the NTS as a Christmas card and borrowed by a major medical drug company for theirs. The NTS kindly gave me life membership for this*).

Two walks during the day and noted that the feeding pattern of the sheep had changed to suit the snow cover. Small spring origin stream temp 46.0 degrees F.

January 11

Sunday. Further snow during the night. The sun quickly clears on the slopes during the day. The sheep used the cleits for warmth and browsed inside the grass tufts. Snow 2" deep in front meadow and in places had drifted to six inches. The first time I have seen them pawing the snow away to get at the grass. More successful Potter trapping on the flushes. PM's on Oystercatcher and Lapwing today. The forecasted Northerly Gale started at 16.00 hours. Film with George Formby in evening.

January 12

Northerly gale had blown its worst between 02.00 and 07.00 hours. I was up in the dark to listen to the test match but interference bad. Big swell but little wind. Walked up to Decca and over to the Old Wall drifted with snow, surrounding the top perimeter of Gleann Mor. Glen Bay looked rough and I visited the Cambir for the first time, sitting in the wind overlooking Soay Stac and Soay itself. Back to the camp at 16.20 after a good 7 mile walk.

January 13

The spares for the thermohydrograph had arrived and I set it up again. More snow overnight, mostly after 07.00 hours. Slow thaw all day. In the PM did a draft on the seals for Morton Boyd, stained a few slides, walked around the village and learnt more Swedish.

January 14

Hope of a thaw today. Still trapping mice. Spring water temp. 47.0 deg F. Continuation of seal report for Morton.

January 15

A morning walk around village in fine weather.

January 16

Fine sunrise at 09.05 hours seemingly just to the left of the middle of the bay when standing on the cliff above the pier. I wrote a few letters to overseas birdwatchers met on islands (*one-upmanship*).

There is now 3" of snow on Am Blaid. I noted the extent of it in Gleann Mor and saw that only in a crescent around the sea edge were the sheep finding some grazing. My return down the road where there was 5" of snow was best done in a series of large leaps. The lorry had failed to get up. The two Woodcock wintering are spending the daytime separately in cleits: their footsteps in the snow give them away, and it's a strange feeling too as they break cover past your right ear!

January 17

A warm front is passing, which suited my two hour ration issue. In PM did a walk and then settled down to a commentary on the rugby against England at Cardiff. A Swedish lesson after tea.

January 18

Sunday. Heavy rain beating on the roof all night. Mist hid the hills while it was still raining heavily (52 mm over these two days). The water is coming down the 'dry burn' in great torrents and water is spouting down the gullies from the tops. Water Rail and Glaucous Gull in the village.

January 19

Worked on the Met. records and then did a blood count on one of the Privates; Haemoglobin, red blood cell count and white blood cells. After lunch did a differential count on the latter. After shifting large stones in the PM my own fingers were bleeding. Who will do my blood count?

January 20

Wind easterly, f. 8–9 E arising during the night, a day after a storm in the Shetlands. During the morning I worked on the maximum and minimum temperatures for the first half of this month using the calculated Index Error. The wind blew harder and opposite on Ruaival streams of water flowing down the slope were reaching the cliff edge and blowing back up the hill. The wind veered to NE and started blowing from the Gap, bringing with it a cloud of fine salt spray formed at the base of Conachair, gusting up the cliff and fleeing across the Conachair slope above the village, and what did not fall there easily cleared Mullach Sgar on the far side. Here was St Kilda in its finest mood, wet, rough, and cold, though not miserable.

January 21

Wind has dropped to f. 7, S. I did some surgery to the wing tip of an immature Herring Gull. I wrote to the Cowglen Quartermaster both officially and a 'wish you were here letter' (he had been here for the hand over). Also wrote one to the Scottish Command Dermatologist.

The ice had all gone off the top and the tups in their clubs were nibbling at the less course heather with lips clear and teeth into action solo. No Fulmars here for days. Probably more Woodcock than I thought but all as singles.

January 22

More snow which quickly cleared when the sun rose. Some photography in the village to record the snow free flushes. At 15.00 hours the wind strengthened and suddenly veered north from NW. Near full moon tonight.

January 23

A lazy day. I put the undercoat on the new Puff Inn sign for the bar, and listened to a concert by the Boston Symphony Orchestra.

January 24

Two hours ration issues and some short odd jobs: they were really parts of long jobs, but it keeps the interest up. The tups are now well clubbed up feeding in the areas with poor nutritional level (*this allows the pregnant ewes with their last year's lambs at heel to forage the better areas*). No Fulmars.

January 25

Sunday. One short walk today and some hours on the plasticine model. Do I miss going to church? No. There is so much around me where He has had a hand in creation, and so much time to meditate, that there is no need.

January 26

Mull due tomorrow and there being six officers expected, I spent some time in getting their accommodation ready. I blancowed my gaiters and dubbined my boots and shoes, and prepared a drum of towels and instruments for sterilisation at Cowglen Military Hospital. In evening a f. 8 S. gale outside, a welcome bath inside, and started reading Dr Zhivago after. *Mull* now unlikely to come.

January 27

Wind has veered from NW to NE and dropped, but there is a big swell. I worked on the pub sign but could have done with some yellow paint to lighten up legs and bill. I finished Dr Z. in bed tonight. A great novel. The only exercise was a walk over to Dun Gap where the low tide exposed the flat topped rocks in it. I sat above a young seal.

January 28

A f. 5–6 wind was too much for the *Mull* and it was from the west, so not coming in to the bay. Further discussion is expected at 18.00 hours.

Now the back of *Fratercula artica* is black, a shiny black, and his chest is glossy white with a dingy area from the earth acquired from digging (*some years later I was to notice that while walking the claw that has to remain sharp is 'deformed' upwards and avoids wear and tear until it is needed in digging*). A walk around the village after tea and then a little more painting. He was given a vermilion eye ring at 21.30 hours. The boat has set out and is due in at 08.00 hours.

January 29

Breakfast at 07.30 hours, but as usual she was going to be later than expected. This gave me time to temporarily mount the Puffin above the bar, and clear enough of my room to make it suitable for the Royal Mail. She arrived in at 09.45 hours making a wide diversion around Levenish as she came into the bay. Wind NW, f. 2, and SW, f. 2 yesterday; and they still won't get their own boat out. Sgt. Murphy RAMC was going off so he was at hand for accidents and I was at the sharp end of the process for getting the cutter into the sea off the low loader. We landed four officers, one a Signals chap, one an Engineer and two waterborne transport RASC officers; one a Capt. Mike Western with great sailing experience who had been on the runs during the summer. Every visitor was clear by 21.30 having been fed well and set about their tasks with energy and understanding.

The cutter had now to be brought in onto the low loader. The tide was full with one wave in ten able to knock any one over. Myself and one other were posted around the corner of the pier with one of the boat's lines to hold. We lost this in an effort to save ourselves, which we did but we were waist deep, and swimming, alternately for fifteen minutes, clinging onto any protruding rock near when the spent wave flowed back, They got a rope to us and we got it onto the boat as she appeared around the corner as if to say 'sorry' with the helpless crew of two having to jump out with ropes on into the water.

With the water up to my shoulders, I was aware that there were two lorries waiting for their turn at the top of the slipway as if they were Huskies waiting for a sledge, and all that was needed from me was to get a clove hitch over any protrusion on the boat, which I did with more ease than anticipated. I waited for a good wave to push me up the slipway and was on the concrete safe. I ordered an issue of rum, had a hot bath and went to a warm bed.

However pleasant and dutiful our visitors were they would have been in a better position to report on the need for a new pier extension if they had had to watch us.

January 30

Do the gods lie awake at night? A day such as today must have been given us as a reward for last night's work, for it was warm all day and my face tingled at night from lying in a chair in the Mess with the sun on it through the open window. Even the sheep slept facing the sun, blinking into it and cudding. There were rafts of Fulmars between us and Boreray but few on Conachair and the Gap. The days are lengthening out.

January 31

I did the second half of the Rations this morning, having been up since 07.00 hours listening to the Australians slowly piling on the runs in the fourth test. Wind f. 5, S. The island lacks green apart from the flushes. Walked to Gap, Lower Conachair and Tobar Childa.

Met. figures for January:

```
Mean 09.00 Temp. at 4ft 6″          40.3 degrees F
Highest Max                         50 degrees F
Lowest Min                          30 degrees F
Lowest Max                          36 degrees F
Highest Min                         48 degrees F
Total Rainfall                      172.9 mm
No of raindays                      25
No of days wind force 8 or more      7
No of days snow lying at station 16
```

Chapter Six

....

Oystercatcher Opening Mussel

Marking Time for the Awakening

February 1

Sunday. I had the benefit of choice today: some stone walling, analysing Met. records since we put up the replacement equipment, walking the village, and 'talking' to Ravens.

February 2

As yesterday but added a Swedish lesson.

February 3

Most diaries start on rising. Today's does but the time was 02.00 hours when the night generator attendant, Gunner King, woke both Tony and myself to tell us that a trawler was in the bay with mail. Wind S, f. 1. I grabbed some waiting mail and we had a quiet sea at ebb tide to get the dory in. Tony Riach fired a Very light to tell them we were coming. What a smooth handover! Tea at 03.00 hours then bed, and up at 07.45 hours to listen to the test match.

February 4

A weak sun shone from a sky clear of cloud but through a weak mist. The tops of the hills were clear but Dun and Levenish hardly visible. The top of Soay was like a smiling schoolboy with a raised cap, showing his tidy glistening hair: the cap held high being a discrete cloud. There were no birds or sheep on the tops, and I only noted the latter at 700ft on the way down. Back in time for elevenses. After lunch I went out with Private Rhodes, a real stalwart, and we counted the sheep making notes as to sex, colour, and probable age.

Later on I started on a village map using a tracing of Matheson's map, Macgregor's (1957) symbols and my own corrections noted on my walks. I did some more repairs to Cleit No. 109 this morning.

February 5

The mice marking continues (*it is strange that when I did come off, the NC did not make it possible for me to pass on my findings to someone who was coming on at their behest to work full time on them*). Curry for lunch but not hot enough. Village walk, I started the ditch for tomorrow's cesspit session and Rhodes finished it. There has been no rain for seven days and the streams have a scanty flow.

The blood supply to Cpl. Cunnah's finger was copious when he cut it in the kitchen, but I stitched the top back on (*it healed well and seen in 1963 was a good result*).

February 6

NAAFI are to take over the supply of rations as from the 1st of March, so an item stock check was needed. Post lunch walk around the village, wrote to the Director of Met. at Edinburgh, restarted the repair of Cleit No. 109, laying the turf on top (the sheep will graze their tops if they can climb up). Started the Ration issue and had a bath to remove the odour factor after the cesspit work this morning.

February 7

Ration issue getting more enjoyable now that I understand the intricate rules. Time taken up this morning transferring eighty pounds of dried egg powder to biscuit tins. The army biscuits have universal use and are excellent. I suggested a small amount of baking powder is added to the scrambled egg to fluff it up. This was well received. I went up to Tobar Childa with a spade and did a few alterations to the water flow with the following in mind: stream is blocked and adjoining surface water is higher; spread of Iris is facilitated; this is advantageous for cover but the delta type vegetational cover might reduce drinking water to birds in dry weather; a few gaps might help observation of skulking birds.

February 8

Sunday. There is no wireless so I played Tchaikovsky's 5th Symphony and the Pomp and Circumstance Marches on the

Gramophone while reading Sunday Times of Jan 18 and 25. This is in anticipation of a trawler during the week. During a gale I usually play Mendelssohn, some of his music swirls but never quite in time with the spray on the roof of the Mess.

February 9

Village rather lifeless today, but I did do a walk at 14.00 hours and within an hour or so the tranquillity of the morning ebb was past and the sea was breaking onto the pier.

February 10

Two or three hours heavy rain at bedtime last night and the wind veered westerly. After breakfast I had a foot inspection and vitamin parade. I can walk up to Am Blaid (¾ mile and c. 700ft) in eighteen minutes, and did so after the parade. This enabled me to get to the rim of Gleann Mor, count the sheep, noticing that they were in groups of less than six, and get back to the MI room in a wee gale, sixty five minutes after starting. In the afternoon at ebb tide most of us helped down at the pier, in a gang, trying to move large boulders from below the slipway using wire hawsers to take the primary pull from a lorry, and a rope controlled telegraph pole swinging derrick to give some aerial control. A semi submerged 12 footer in the *Laminaria* zone had to be split, but we got one half out before the tide turned.

February 11

The magnitude of the sea this morning was far in excess of the only local cause, a southerly gale here. After lunch I walked along the boulder strewn shore, away from the sandy part, from the pier in order to photograph the seas coming in, while the tide was ebbing. This was expected to be the safest time, and it was, bar one moment when my search for an artistic spectacle clashed with a wave that wished to use me as a spectacle of power. One large rock saved me from immersion higher than my waist, but needing to have my camera held high was a hindrance.

February 12

It was catch up day in the MI room mainly with furnishings and rescue equipment. It blew about f. 8, S. all day and the seas went across the mouth of the bay like race horses with outstretched necks.

February 13

The low cloud over the hills and a fine steady drizzle, not entirely composed of freshwater, make it a real St Kilda day, and during the early hours of the evening the wind rose to f. 9, being f. 8 at the time the morning met. readings were sent to Benbecula.

By lunch time we had cleared some mess up in the ward, and distributed odd bits of metal for which we either knew no use, foresaw no use, or had no use, around the MI room, hanging from the ceiling, hidden behind cupboards, and in odd corners. No doubt if these are found hidden, perhaps elsewhere, learned historians will class them as either 13th C or RAMC.

During the afternoon I started issuing two weeks rations with Private Rhodes, and did a stock take. A quick walk around the village at 16.30 hours showed the sheep huddled against the walls as the rain swept across the street. This is the weather they hate. I can't say we enjoy it, but we still thrive.

February 14

Cloud cover has thinned. I spent the whole morning in the Ration stores. An hour after lunch I went up to the Gap via the enclosures. No Fulmars. My return was interrupted by a Lowestoft trawler, LO 427 *Robert Hewit* coming into the bay, answering neither morse or RT. Where are the seafaring manners of East Anglia? A session in the bar tonight after some MI room work. The medics are in charge of the bar.

February 15

Sunday. The sun arose around Oiseval's shoulder and the wind had dropped. Mouse trap collection after breakfast, and with the sad absence of wireless and newspaper, I read and wrote in the MI room. Before lunch with the window wide open I sat in the sun. After lunch I went up to the quarry with the wind at my stern, and sat and watched into Gleann Mor, then walking so I could look onto the adjoining slopes of Conachair, where there were about 6000 Fulmars cackling and fencing. Warm frontal conditions starting on my return.

February 16

I worked at the final Ration list all morning. Ambient temp. was 52 deg. F and I went around Oiseval in the afternoon. The paths are intriguing, because it is difficult to see above and below the one you have chosen, but each has junctions chosen by the sheep. The tendency is to walk up and less often go down. The sward is short and the exposed areas rough and easy to walk on if one can bear the lack of perception.

During the next few weeks I continued to map these paths so that they could go onto my model. There are Wrens here that

have long lost their alarm calls, never having seen a human,
and their only defiance is to come very close and sing.

February 17

'Fronts in General' is the title of the present book being read:
and for the second time I try to see a three dimensional moving
space in order to understand it. The *Mull* is due on Thursday,
but her arrival depends on the fronts, and two Brigadiers will
be inspecting our fronts and backs, so the Medical rooms were
cleaned and tidied.

Curry for lunch and afterwards it was pile and count, count
and pile a great number of empty sacks of many shapes and
varying degrees of 'holiness' in a large heap so that no one in
his senses would ever dream of counting them. Afterwards I
moved three sacks of gravel from the dry burn to patch the
path up from the slipway after a few more obstinate jagged
stones had been removed, probably having fallen off the wall,
which now looked better as a grass covered bank.

I did some washing and ironing, and after tea removed
some stains off the Officers' Mess floor, when, having got my
hand thoroughly dirty, thought it the right moment to dubbin
my boots. Bath was then the only place to remove it, and
although hasty, it was welcome. Film in the evening.

February 18

We spent this morning tidying up the laboratory, and during
the afternoon Sergeant finished the central reception room,
and Rhodes and myself did the toilet, finding probably our last
treasure trove in a large box as yet only half opened, containing
about two dozen jars of ammonium sulphate. Enough to test
the urines for ketones (*present in out of control diabetics, and*

starvation) of every soldier here once a week for eight years. There should be enough.

Then I walked the village. The female sheep are now quite predominant in the village, there hardly being more than half a dozen males present this afternoon. The ewes were 'touchy' which should mean they are strangers from higher up who have come down sensing better grazing. The tups are in a low state higher up.

During the evening the wind blew up and any hopes of the *Mull* coming tomorrow became less. Not until our flag hangs loose in abandoned despair do they consider venturing out.

February 19

RT from *Mull* at 07.00 hours told us they would not consider it. They were right as it is f. 9 now. I walked up to the quarry via stream and village. After tea I carried on with Madame Bovary (reading her!)

After the evening film I sat down with Pt. George Maclellan and wrote down all the Gaelic names used on the island as he pronounced them, in my own personal phonetic spelling. George is very bright.

February 20

The wind had veered NW overnight but still blew strongly. A placid bay with hardly a ruffle to my hair. I worked on the maps in the morning and in the afternoon walked up to the Gap where I lay on the turf inhaling the vision as thrown before me. Boreray, tall dark, and slowly becoming engulfed by a hail storm crossing from the left, held its head high, never glancing in its aloofness at the waves leaping up at its feet like white freshly entered puppies. The wind swept the sea strongly and

Fulmars sped downwind before gliding back skilfully using the troughs as shelter. Cliff clamour there was none: all for the eyes and none for the ears. A routine return via the village.

After tea I finished off Madame Bovary. So did the author: with arsenic.

February 21

To write of swirling clouds around the island would not be correct for they merely hung, but with such density that I can with truth write that it was the worst day for visibility yet, but still not a fog. Continuous drizzle and great puffs of cloud squashed our mighty hills into insignificance. The fleeces of the brown sheep glistened, but our appreciation was more than theirs. It was a day for indoor jobs and if we had sails we would be becalmed.

At 14.30 hours the *Mull* left from her safe anchorage in thick fog, flag flying limply from her mast, minus a Brigadier who had flown back to Edinburgh in premature despair, with several emetical persons.

I went to bed at 19.30 hours in preparation for an early rise.

February 22

Sunday. At 03.00 hours I rose from my 'pit' and after a bacon and egg breakfast of sufficient magnitude to keep me stoked up for a few hours felt great. Those who had got the raft down to the pier to be tied up were experiencing some nasty buffeting, and of course it was still dark. At 04.00 hours the *Mull* came in, very slowly, rather timorously, and with flickering lights.

Such was the swell that we had to signal that a delay was to be expected due to the irregular action of the dory engine in the water. At 07.30 hours the first people were landed, not too worse for the trip, but too late for the nice warm beds we had made up for them in the Factor's House. Col. Cooper, Major Francis, and Capt. Warner the new CO had arrived and a NAAFI man to whom I was to hand over the Rations to on behalf of the RASC. All breakfasted and then started work. Lunch at 11.00 hours and at noon we were again working, but soon I was able to look through my mail and answer the important letters. Dad sent some wonderful feminine bar paintings, and after supper, with the approval of my Sgt., they were put up in the Canteen (*these later provoked several remarks about the Doc. and his female patients*). Once the tide again obliged, we started offloading again, and I loaded Ration Stores onto the lorry which were in excess of our needs.

At 17.30 hours those who were returning took supper and at 18.15 hours we saw the last visitor onto the cutter off the raft. I then took my turn on the raft, which was used as a landing platform for the offloading of the wood, and in the periods of rest my heavy but buoyant platform, which we had built of telegraph poles and diesel drums in the autumn, rocked gently in the swell, the guiding rope slipping occasionally through my hands in the bigger waves to return in the troughs.

It was now dark and when the cutter was ready we had her around the corner and onto the trolley, and in record time had her up the slipway, followed by the raft. Supper at 20.30 hours, a few hours at the bar and then bed.

February 23

A day of sorting, creating a new Ration Book, and re-arranging. Took a village and enclosure walk: very dull. A 21st birthday party of some magnitude in the Canteen. We have a wonderful pair of cooks who give 24 hour cover, produce meals at the time they are needed on their own initiative, delight in their routine and any special event, and advise me on my decisions and suggestions, without embarrassing my senior role (*I kept in touch with them post National Service*).

February 24

The hills were once again draped in mist, and as heavy as the clouds hung, so also did as many eyelids. My hospital training held me in good stead; regular night work and limited alcohol. I finished off the Ration work, and after lunch walked up the road in heavy rain, taking occasional shelter in the cleits. After tea caught up with my paper reading (am now reading Feb 7). Bath and then film.

How does the island look in February? Frankly the deadest month yet, but the Fulmars are now coming back more frequently. The Starlings, sitting around in pairs on the cleits, exercising their laryngeal muscles with great effect, appear to be a little more conscious of future propagational duties, and the grass grows green where sheep have lain, sharing some warmth with the earth and returning nutrients to it from the vegetation they nosed for and nibbled during bleaker weeks. The tups, as if guilty of previous promiscuity in the autumn (*no chance of this in the village anyhow as Frederick even put dominance before food*) wander alone or in small groups, lean, shaggy, and lethargic like spent Salmon, while the cause of their revels; about a hundred agile, fat and nervy females, browse the village pastures, some with shaggy yearling lambs still a'heel, and at least one with twins still wandering close. On these rest the future of the population for the coming year. In these exist '*foetuses*' in a constant state of anoxia equivalent to twenty times the height of Conachair, soon to breathe air on experiencing their first most important sensory stimulus, that of a knock on the face. A facial smack which sparks into action the motor portion of the respiratory centre in the brain.

Bleak are the hills, strong the winds and wet the air, but still higher is the arc of the sun over Dun and even now clearing Mullach Sgar, no longer to cast its weak light only on cliffs. A few seals lie on Dun very inactive, and Gulls wander amongst them picking up the refuse but still with a listening ear for the clank of the dustbins being emptied off the pier. There are few trawlers, an ever boisterous sea, and still isolation. But all are happy.

February 25

The wind was high, the air hung wet, and I sat in the MI room starting the February weather report. These are strictly climatological records, and my thrice daily observations go to Benbecula airport and are one of many sources from which the shipping forecast are made and which I listen to at 08.00 hours when I get up. A very low tide was expected at 13.30 hours, and as we wanted to clear more rocks we all had lunch early. The wind increased causing a small flock of Oystercatchers on the beach to balance their piebald bodies by shifting their feet. The village sheep allowed the wind to enforce a gentle trot with their hindquarters acting as a sail. At 16.00 hours the wind became SW, f. 10 to 11 for two hours, shaking the buildings.

This was after a warning from Benbecula that we were to expect 35 knots. Our variety hurled stacked doors into the air over the telephone wires.

February 26

Another blustery day. After lunch I walked up to the Gap and watched the Fulmars gliding over the waves. The sun broke through intermittently and suddenly it shone brilliantly on Boreray and the Stacs to show a thousand Gannets on the nearest stack and about three thousand in all. It was as if they were being presented from behind a curtain. With the glasses they were white dots four miles away.

I followed the bay facing edge of Conachair around until the small pools at Tobar Childa (Well of Kilda) came into view. These are fed by surface and spring water so the whole area is now spongy wet. Soon after tea we heard a trawler hooting. I wrote a quick letter home and then sealed the mail bag. The lads got the boat out by engine and oars to the *Margaret Wick* and returned with mail and fish. They awaited a quiet period and then pulled on the buoy rope to the pier. Their bow rope was out now with engine off, and the stern rope followed and with several people scampering along the quay, we got her as far as the corner when a huge wave came in, filled her and threw her up into the air. Two lads jumped out into the water and in a few seconds we had her around the corner of the pier.

There was just time for a bath before supper, even having opened my mail, and an hour and a half or so later she slipped out into a stormy night, with the wind force dropping.

February 27

I went to bed this morning at 01.15 hours having worked on the Met. recording and at last finished it.

At 09.00 hours I started organised treatment for five people with 'Athletes foot' or *Tinea pedis*, a fungus infestation. The wind blew f. 8 all morning and the cloud was low and thick, however it was not to touch Conachair until mid afternoon, when after making good way up the road to the Marconi set on Mullach Mor it was stronger from the SW. Boreray was quite hidden, and thin cloud came rushing over the Mullach Mor/Conachair col with tremendous speed. The Radar bowl shook and swung. After a quick glimpse into Glen Bay, I staggered towards Conachair and turned into the wind, the salty air beating onto my face, and when my mouth was opened and my head turned at an angle to the wind, one cheek filled out and the other sunk in to the *buccal* cavity, making me a schizofacial individual, seemingly presenting as Cushing's Syndrome on one side and peptic ulceration on the other.

It was probably blowing f. 12 to 13 up there and the effects did not diminish until quarry level, where I turned left across the graveyard, getting back by 15.00 hours. The sea got up higher in the evening.

February 28

The last day of February and Rations day: but it took me less time than expected. With less wind and some sunshine I was able to sow more grass seed. The last lot has been showing for a few days and has done quite well. I returned to the Mess and read, and then ate a large lunch, after which I lay in the arm chair in hot dazzling sun listening to 'Take it from here'. The two international matches were on at 15.00 hours and setting off to the village in shoes I was suddenly seized with a strong urge to climb up Conachair (1396ft) via Glacan Conachair, partly because it was a wonderful day, and partly because I had an urge, hard to resist, to appear at the top above the two slow climbers who, having seen me at one of their stops were 400 yards to the right. I had left the Factor's House at 13.55 hours, at 15.10 hours I was back listening to the rugby, having climbed 1300ft plus, had five minutes break sitting on the bed of Woodrush at the top, and come straight down.

There were as many Gannets around Boreray as on the 26th, and Fulmars at sea but not around the cliffs.

Met. figures for February:

```
Mean 09.00 hrs
  Temp @ 4ft 6"      47.3 degrees F
Highest Max          52.0 degrees F on
                       10, 14, 16, 27, 28th
Mean max             49 degrees F
Lowest Min           39 degrees F on 3rd
Lowest Max           44 degrees F on 6th
Highest Min          50 degrees F on 16th, 22nd
Greatest rainfall in a day   8.6 mm on 13th
Total for month              62.2 mm
Number of rain days > 0.2 mm 15
Number of rain days > 1.0 mm 13
Number of days hail            1
Number of days with wind
  force 8 or more             15
```

March 1

Sunday. Having now been here six months, perhaps a few thoughts on paper from the assortment in my mind would be appropriate, for six months life here with partial isolation should leave some kind of mark, and indeed it has, but mainly through activities both physical and mental, which have occupied the potential vacuum so created by position and circumstances. My first impressions are now firmly implanted, and those that were a novelty are now admitted into my life without further thoughts. Even so they never fail to give satisfaction and still thrill me, whether it be the sight of a huge rolling sea (from the land) with scurrying clouds of wind whipped spray, the sound of a wave which having lost its momentum on the beach, failing to wreak the destruction intended, withdraws, rolling the stones with an ugly growl, while awaiting another 'go', or the continual sense dulling wind on the face when walking or crawling into a gale. All these and more are weekly events. Others, such as the never boring jagged outline of Dun, and the mighty cliffs of Conachair, contrast with the sanctity of the village street. These are constant companions.

I have not thought of men, for thoughts mellow and conceptions change, but of the wintering party of twenty five there are three or four who can look at the island as a bonus visit in their National Service. Others see us as on a rock whose limits are wet and stormy, and only too ready to prove a barrier to escape by boat back to the land of Public Houses, motor bikes, and the opposite sex: where mice have to be put up with, where sheep behave like goats, and where getting the Royal Mail involves hard work and more wetness than could be provided anywhere else in the process of posting and receiving letters.

To some it is an escape from harsh realities of life; self invented or by the deeds of others (*those whom I have met up with since relived their tales with comfort*). What is it to me? That can be gleaned from these diaries so far. The novelty is still there at base, but the growth in the attraction of the situation is steady and must persist. City bustle is far away and almost dreaded. My friends are sometimes further, and are missed, but letters go between us and friendships continue without obligation. Two soldiers correctly asked me as Postmaster to write a note he could send to his girl certifying that he was where he said he was and not in Fleetwood (where the mail was posted by the trawler crews).

Above all these negative feelings the pulse of St Kilda for ever beats, regular and full, perhaps with a few geriatric signs in the village. There are signs of a slowly awakening seasonal sea life, a sea which, in the weeks to come will slow down the increasing warmth of the land, just as she has kept us warm during the winter. The sea has no rest and seeks none. She dances with Caribbean fervour but without the sun, for she is now part of the NE flowing Gulf steam many miles from her origin off mid America, where the sun heated her quiet tropical waters before sending them off our way past the cold Labrador current as far as the North Cape, Bear Island, Svalbard, and around the tip of Greenland where the Vikings used it; but more importantly to us, preventing us being like South Georgia.

Today the sea danced in uncontrolled anguish, and the wind urged her on. I spent the morning reading a newspaper three weeks old. Quiet village walk in afternoon with less energy than there was in the sea and wind.

March 2

It seems that I did the February Met. summary this morning and only got half way through (*but it must be remembered that I had no calculation gadgets other than above my neck and ten fingers*).

No seals on Dun for ten days.

March 3

It rained all last night and I walked up through An lag Bho'n Tuath (meaning 'the Northern Valley') to note how many Fulmars were there. There were about three thousand around the Gap, many of which were on ledges, with the nearer pairs fencing and gapping at each other, uttering loud calls pleasant to the human ear, but intoxicating to other Fulmars.

After a little post tea Swedish, I walked to the signals centre. To my right some fat ewes grazed among the cleits: but with the addition of a wet lamb standing shakily with the shock of being *ex utero*. It was wandering behind a pale Langhan type ewe, but was itself dark. Mother was probably two years old (*experience later with my own sheep confirms the weakness in the bond with those younger ewes, and the plaintiff calls of the lamb trying to follow mum through the houses were infrequently answered; and when they were replied to, seemed more like a 'shut up'. Most Soay ewes have last year's young also around and once I witnessed a ewe a year old lambing, with her mother doing the cleansing*).

March 4

I 'did' the mice and Met. first. Yesterday's lamb looked fit with a good bond, and there were two more with dark parents. The tup that was found in the same area had been dead 24 hours, so I went back to the camp for a knife and by 11.45 hours had skinned him and removed the viscera. After lunch I did an extensive post mortem examination.

As expected there was very little subcutaneous fat and no omental fat. Patchy consolidation one lung and a little oedema. Some oedema of larynx and vocal chords, and naso pharynx oedematous with mucous. Heart, trachea, liver, spleen, pancreas normal, a few nematode worms in gut, stomach full, kidneys a little pale, no mesenteric calcification, brain too soft to examine. Cause of death: upper respiratory infection with pneumonia. It was as if the sight of his own progeny gave the sign: mission complete. Apparently there are nine small lambs on Am Blaid up top.

March 5

At 09.30 I started up to Am Blaid up the road, but the one toner picked me up. Once I could see into Glen Bay and Gleann Mor, I was able to do a count of sheep and found four lambs in sixty two sheep with few males amongst them. Walking along the old bank/wall I went as far as the Lover's stone on the west cliffs from where I could look up to Mullach Bi (1164ft) and down to the great talus slope of Carn Mor. On the grassy slopes below me were eleven sheep, five of which had lambs.

I returned over Loch Sgar, crossed the road, walked around the edge of the flat plateau and back towards Decca. I could see no sheep on Ruaival and returned via the diesel dump.

After lunch I did some inorganic chemistry, trying to find the strength of the Johnson Acid Fixol by titration with iodine, using starch as an indicator. I did some write up work after the film.

March 6

Tiny bunches of cumuli permitted the sun to shine most of the morning, and even with a north wind, it was warm. At 09.30 hours I set off for the Gap and spent some time proving that a direct association between the centre of the Fulmar's vertical and horizontal swoops were indeed based on the ledge it had chosen and sat on. Rather as expected really but with so many birds so close – it was not easy.

The first Meadow Pipits have arrived, on their way north. Another sowing of grass seed carried out. At 14.55 I went around Oiseval behind the camp. The 'around' is half a mile long and 900ft high but from this subtract 200ft of steep cliff coming up from the sea.

I summarise a very detailed account of these slopes. There are four gullies and five ridges, the first and last being fused with a large high rock above. The second and third gullies are climbable, the fourth leads up to the last ridge which fuses with the high rock on its right. From here complex sheep paths lead around and it was possible to find other end points where failure to proceed had arisen before, and where one was in relation to the next one; and one can emerge at the top and be put off by a 20ft rock face, which it is possible to pass. The whole slope is a maze of paths which some sheep use, almost getting down to a point 100ft above the high tide level, of flat area 18 acres in all. Very rarely can one stand upright without using a steadying hand.

I got back to camp at 16.20 hours.

March 7

The morning was almost fully occupied issuing the rations, but I now have a good system working and it is much less trouble. We have only ever had one set of complaints and that was when the Spanish trawlers bought us enough crab for a week; as soup, as cold and as a hot dish. It only suited the two officers. No. 1 lamb was found today at Cleit No. 114, looking for its mum who was at Cleit No. 119. Both were bleating and neither made much attempt to unify the two bleats.

I encouraged the lamb towards her and when recognition was positive, smartly hid. Probably this aloofness has developed in this habitat because of the absence of quadruped predators.

After 15.00 hours I walked to the Gap and onto Oiseval from that side. Rather a riotous evening in the bar.

March 8

Sunday. My Sunday paper of Feb. 22, purposely not read last Sunday, came in useful today. It was still unfinished when the *St Bardolph* came into the bay during 'Your Concert Choice'.

This boat is not our favourite. Last week she came as far as the mouth of the bay and turned back. This was the boat that came in very late after Christmas and grumbled. A few weeks later she came in at 02.00 hours, and now she has come at low tide, and anchored as near Ireland as is possible in the bay. This time the dory was soon down, but against a moderate sea, and she was twice thrown high when on the buoy. The crew got her there in twenty minutes and back in fifteen, with some fish as compensation.

The sea was now rather heavier and they waited on the buoy holding on to the 20 yard rope to the quay for 4 to 5 minutes. At last they decided to pull themselves in through the swirling fronds of *Laminaria*, and two successive waves lifted them up and threw them down with equal velocity onto the boulders at the entrance. The boat straddled the largest and was soon half full of water, so that most of the crew jumped out and were up to their shoulders in water. About twelve of us were pulling on the line and ropes to get her in, and eventually succeeded, but as exciting and courageous all this is, as resuscitation officer I was still involved in the wet work, and felt that more of us should wear lifejackets.

All being well this boat will be at Fleetwood on Friday so I was able to get a quick note off telling them of my planned leave. The next few hours before and after lunch were spent going through my mail, which included letters from Capt. Dorothy Savage QARANC, Dr Joan McBroom, and a family of Russian Émigrés, the Vassiljews (White Russians) who I had cared for in a hush hush unit in Fife.

A quick village walk, a book on Wingate's troops, and a film in evening.

March 9

Wind blowing fiercely when I awoke and strengthened all day, due to an anticyclone over northern Europe and a depression in the Denmark Strait. F. 9 to 10, SSE in the evening.

I worked in the MI room in the morning and sorted tinned potatoes in the afternoon.

At 15.00 hours George, my cook from a South Uist croft, climbed Oiseval with me to help sort the 'geography' out. The wind tore across the summit and we had to push every foot of the way. We climbed down to Cnoc na Gaoith (Windy ridge) and returned another way.

March 10

Cloud that in the morning just hid the tops, by the evening hung low across the quarry. During the afternoon I walked through the village to where the wall meets the bed of Amhuinn Mhor (Big River) and saw two sandy tups nosing amongst the grass. One carried a formidable pair of horns, and there was the same grey muzzle that in the autumnal chases was pushed out, twisted and lowered with a flickering tongue at would be Soay rulers following in a line at a discreet distance behind him. But now heavy hung the head, and how gaunt and fleshless was the body, and bent the hind quarters. This is due to poor feeding but mainly due to reduced androgen secretion, from shrunken testicles, a seasonal expectant but with little hope of recovery in one so old, and in fact with his genes now in the new lambs, it could be thought of as a sad but fortuitous position. The head that raised soft eyes in anticipation will soon hang down for good. I have always called him Frederick. The younger males are in better condition, and mostly in tup clubs.

The females, mostly with last year's ewe lamb at heel, but now more often also with a new lamb, are on their toes and a little twitchy, with head held high, ears turned forward and always ready for a 'scamper'.

What of the newcomers? Most walk with stiff stilted legs, feed from the same warm figure whose smell and appearance are imprinted on them, and lie with feet turned in doze while their dams work at the scanty grass.

March 11

Yet another morning with low blanket cloud and moderate rain. I did some serious plasticine modelling, depicting cliffs, went a quick walk around the village, read some Swedish, and settled down to a book on the history of naval warfare.

March 12

Clouds were lifting from dawn. At 09.30 hours I started up to Am Blaid and got there at 10.00 hours. The NW wind was being funnelled up the north Glen. I walked up as far as the Lover's stone and made topographical notes of the surrounding cliffs for my model. My return to Decca was devoid of lambs but I saw one in the village which was sitting by a senior tup, a bearded and horned 'brute', and then rather suddenly missed the presence of the maternal warm and cuddly creature it had known so well. Quick departure!

Tony Riach had predicted a gale and bet on one. He is now claiming one even though I knew it had sped up to Fair Isle and missed us.

There follows yet another detailed exploration of the Oiseval tracks lasting 2¼ hrs, which enabled the writer to get to a point where he looked up at the Gap from below.

There was an artistic hail storm this afternoon with an opening like a storm of dried peas. After the film in the evening I worked at the model, concentrating on the map I had made when I walked during the day. The hooting of a trawler brought me to a halt. She appeared around Oiseval and we fired a Very light to tell them of our readiness. Our boat was easily launched and soon the mail was with us. Mine was interesting but not copious: interesting because a not very close 'ex' had sent a cutting from Peterborough in the Telegraph mentioning this island unit. The last para. mentioned the Puffin Club, and the Puffin tie.

March 13

At breakfast it was blowing f. 8 over the island of Dun which is immediately over the bay from the Mess, and by mid afternoon it was causing a very big sea which was thundering in with a f. 9 behind it. By 20.00 hours both had increased further and the medical room was twisting and bending on its foundations, now certainly f. 10. The MI room was making noises as if in pain from the torture it was enduring. It was hard to distinguish rain from sea spray, but most of the airborne sea spray had a maritime origin anyhow. At 21.30 hours or thereabouts, nine of us went out to move the dory higher; it was quite a weight, but the wind had found no difficulty, for even though left upside down this 12ft boat was lifted up and flung over on its side with a bang that brought people out of the Sergeants' Mess. The pier was now almost permanently engulfed in spray, and the lamp rocked to and fro on its sentinel perch, lighting up the waves breaking over it. My neck and face stung in the salt, and the return of my body to the MI room with a following wind was suggestive of a hidden means of jet propulsion.

The clouds hung lower and just before midnight, while negotiating the stepping stones across the enclosure to the Factor's House where the officers slept, the warm, wet, and salty wind, blew from over the storm beaten sea; audible but quite hidden in the spray and darkness.

March 14

Troubles and storms soon blow over, and the morning was quiet compared to last night's gale. Nothing has really prevented my village walk, though some have been short. A hiding migrant would be there by the walls, in the reed beds or even the roofless houses. I had learnt this on Fair Isle and Skokholm, the former with a school friend medical student and the latter with my botany master from Oundle School. Birds recorded in foul conditions always stick in the mind. This time I returned in time for the Ireland v Wales rugby match.

At around 23.00 hours I started up the road on the way to Carn Mor, a talus slope on the west cliffs under Mullach Bi, on the far side of the island, for if Shearwaters were present, with the dropped wind, and crescent moon, conditions seemed right. I had little hope that I would arrive to find Manx Shearwaters crashing into the rocks around me, but a glorious negative result would be valuable.

At 23.40 I got to Am Blaid and strode off to the embankment around the top of the Glen, stumbling and sliding on wet grass towards Mullach Bi, which stood over the great talus slope as father and mother of its creation. I found the 'indicator cleit', walked and slid down the path I found in daylight, and twisted around the bottom end of the buttress. Ahead a sheep stirred, dazzled by my torchlight, as if guilty of being in the barren 'rock garden' wisely decided not to run on the hidden terrain.

For some time I sat. The clouds slowly drifted overhead, threatening showers. Silence reigned. The sea below was white but shone not. In all it was decidedly unromantic.

Climbing up towards the cliff face above me boulders as big as small houses, with spaces below them large enough to hold a dozen or more people, continually interrupted my progress. Turning right I followed the ridge down again, went around it and with extended fingers and inverted feet, found it a slow but steady return to the top. Soon the lights of the camp shone and at 02.10 hours I was in bed.

March 15

Sunday. A sunny day for a village walk. A small lamb had lost contact with mum and was selecting other possibilities which harmlessly included me and I politely refused. Not so polite were the young tups who took objection to being nibbled in certain impolite places.

Many years later when trying to feed 'tiddler' lambs on the bottle I discovered that the lambs would not accept it from a male but would from a female. The discernment is made by the lamb by smelling 'certain body areas'.

Mother and lamb met up when she condescended to reply. After lunch I went with George Maclellan to the Gap to explain some Fulmar psychology to him.

March 16

I went with George to Tobar Childa where I eviscerated the sheep I had found dying yesterday, and did a full examination. There was a 3" foetal lamb *in utero* fully formed, but with no other gross changes except for a few endocardial petechial haemorrhages and free fluid in the abdomen. Village walk showed there to be five lambs all in good health, but one in constant trouble in losing ma.

After tea I completed my Swedish question paper, and then had some darts tuition.

March 17

It looked a promising day with great white but harmless clouds hanging over the tops. I got half a lift up to the top and was soon looking down onto Glen Bay. Beyond was the Island of Soay with a 'woolly hat' of orographic cloud. I continued over the top onto Glacan Mor, finding a rocky niche which fitted my posterior and viewed a panorama well familiar but never quite the same. I returned due south over the col and onto Glacan Conachair with a deeply furrowed sharp rocky return to the camp. The sun shone on the rocks and warmed the air gusting up to the top, allowing the cloud to thin. At least one new lamb behind the Factor's House. The *Mull* has left Cairnryan.

March 18

A day in which much time was spent tidying up and preparing for tonight's arrival of the *Mull*, for she left Loch Boisdale at 08.00 hours with as calm a sea as could be asked for. Yesterday's new lamb died just after lunch. It was a quiet death. Mother spent much of the time near him but his flat almost motionless body did not provide the stimulus for perfect motherhood.

The *Mull* came in just before 19.00 hours, the same time as a deep sea trawler swooped in and out of the bay. She was unloaded in perfect conditions. My relief Lieut. Stewart arrived with two REME officers and an Education Corps officer.

March 19

The Ides of March. We left in the morning on a rather misty day with no facilities for those departing. I was well covered but it was a cold journey with my experience getting me to where I could sit with my back to the funnel which was warm. However to compensate, the sea went over my boots each time she rolled. A slow foggy journey through the Sound of Harris.

George is going to do sheep counts while I am off and the medics do as best they can with the Met. reports.

Met. figures for March:

```
Mean 09.00 Temp
  at 4ft 6"        46 deg F
Highest Max        52 on 22nd. Mean max 47
Lowest Min         40 on 7th and 8th. Mean min 45
Lowest Max         41 on 7th
Highest Min        50 on 29th
Greatest rainfall in a day    17.9 on 11th
Total rainfall               90.5 mm
Number of rain days < 0.2 mm 20
Number of wet days < 1.0 mm  16
Number of hail days           2
Number of days gale
  force 8 or more             5
```

Chapter Seven

Puffin

The Return and Reawakening

The journey from St Kilda had been very uncomfortable, sitting on the deck sharing the warmth of the funnel and boiler of the *Mull*, while the boat heaved and plunged in the swell with the sea washing over our feet (*at the time it was a SE 25 knot wind on Hirta*). Four cold, damp, nauseated soldiers sat it out oblivious to the sea and land scenery in the mid distance.

We landed in the dark at Loch Carnan on South Uist and spent the night at the Officers' Mess on Benbecula. Next morning I had seen the Met. Officer to whom I had been sending my reports, and soon after 15.00 hours caught the plane to Renfrew, a journey which took an hour.

That evening at Cowglen we had a little party and the Mess President asked some 'Q A' lasses over. Yes, nurses are good companions! Next day I went to Edinburgh to stay with Col. Ross Henderson, the Dermatologist for Scottish Command. He knew his whiskies. I went to St Mary's Episcopal Church to re-establish the set approved Godly connection on Sunday.

On Monday I went home and during the next two and a half weeks I visited the two Birmingham Hospitals I had worked at, seeing old friends, arranged a GP job for August, saw elderly relatives, bought several books, acquired more photographic equipment, went to a point to point, was welcomed by my bank, consulted my stock broker, and went to Oxford to read at the Edward Grey/BTO Library, saw Ken Williamson who had been interpreting my coded messages, reluctantly tidied and sorted at home and lavished myself with good food.

I recall two island connected events: explaining to an aunt that I had not had any swimming for pleasure, and explaining to a policeman in Princes Street, Edinburgh that my prolonged position staring at a traffic light was due to not having seen RED for a long time, and why. He believed me, and when asked told me what the new lines meant that had recently been painted on the road.

My return journey started on Friday the 10th of April with a train journey to Glasgow, and yet another party at the QARANC Mess at Cowglen Hospital, before my departure from Buchanan Street to Oban on the Saturday. Good dinner in poor hotel: church in the morning and did some painting of the harbour from the hill. Down to the Claymore after supper and found my cabin, where I turned in, and when I awoke found myself well up the Sound of Mull. Coll and Tiree both called at – calves hoisted ashore at one, and one came off the other. The usual crowd at each pier. The swell of the Minch drove me below, and I was glad to be able to take a walk at

Castlebay, Barra. Eventually in the gathering gloom we landed at Lochboisdale in the pouring rain.

I spent from Tuesday to Saturday on Benbecula working on NAAFI stores, comparing the local dances with the Fair Isle and Midland versions, eating well, going over to the Met. Office, and reading. On Saturday morning our Land Rover ploughed through a foot of water at South Ford to get us onto the LCT. Capt. Ian Tweedie was the skipper of the same boat that I had come in when I arrived. Captain Ellis Royal Signals and I were the only officers on the passage.

We reached Hirta at 22.00 hours on the Saturday night after quite a pleasant journey through the Sound of Harris, but decided to anchor in the bay and beach in the morning. However, about midnight we dragged our anchor in the SE swell and all but broke our stern on Dun: gongs sounded and voices hollowed into the darkness as the engines turned the screws that thrashed the white foam on the rocks.

In fact it was our Signals Officer passenger who noted the change of note, looked over the side in his night clothes and shouted 'we are on the rocks' and ran down to change into uniform.

We spent the rest of the night turning circles in the bay, and when I woke found we were firmly anchored in Glen Bay, having looked at the beach at 07.00 hours and decided on a retreat to a familiar hide out. Here we lay the whole day tossing and twisting while I eat little and slept a lot, occasionally glimpsing out into the murky gloom around us. Thus it was that my arrival this morning, the 20th, was welcome and well due.

My first job was to attend to someone on the boat with a dental abscess that had burst during the night and was continuing to drain well and copiously. The LCT left at lunch time with the last three toner having a very wet send off, finally seizing up and floating ten yards from the ramp, with a crowd of rather upset soldiers inside including my relief. The vehicle was finally winched onto the Tank Deck. My lunch went down very well and during the rest of the day I slipped into my routine.

April 21

My first job was to get the Ration situation sorted out, besides doing the Met. The whole morning was spent stocktaking and copying out the book, and this rather tiresome job took me into the afternoon, when I was able to get a lift up top. Deliberately I took a slow devious walk down and noted some awakening: patches of new green grass, more lambs frisking around (as the Psalmist says: *'The mountains skipped like Rams, and the little hills like young sheep'*) and a few primroses out. A pale tup had had his own *Nunc dimittis servum tuum, Domine* in Cleit No. 12. Thin and wasted, I removed his 'crown of horns'. Drumming Snipe heard after dark. Surely this is the Reawakening and Resurrection.

April 22

I spent all morning doing the rations and AQMS Dedman produced a repair method for the secondary spool on my camera while George Mac went around the village with me taking notes on the sheep phenotypes. The lambs were playing in groups, running amok at the slightest excuse, which confused the count somewhat.

We extended our search from sheep to Puffins. None were seen on Hirta but from Ruaival we could see birds flying up and down the ungrazed slopes of Dun, being joined by birds on the sea and standing outside holes. I spent an hour with George in the evening working on the careful sheep and Fulmar notes he had taken in my absence.

April 23

I spent many hours working on the Rations, assuming we will be at a strength of thirty six at peak during the summer, constructing a set of alternatives based on our issues. The Yellow Flag Irises were growing well and it is in this kind of habitat that I hoped to find the 'Leaf Warbler' I thought I saw yesterday, so I took half an hour off my food duties.

April 24

Early to bed last night and set my alarm to go off at 01.30 hours to get me up for the second nocturnal visit of the year to Carn Mor, the big boulder slope under Mullach Bi on the far west side of the island. George Mac was coming with me and we set off under a bright full moon at 02.15 hours. Although this made walking easy I anticipated that there would be fewer birds, for on other Shearwater islands they avoid coming in on light nights. We went the way I have been before in day and night, and got around the buttress without any trouble. I heard the first 'Manxy' swooshing overhead and then heard that lovely call coming from deep down under a boulder, many of which were the size of cottages, and all of which leaned crazily on one another. They called gently to their loved ones below or called to a potential mate above. One or two scuttled for cover as we approached but we caught a few and ringed them. Others were still below us when we had already climbed down 18 feet. Some Fulmars and a predatory Gull were present. At 04.30 hours we started back, George negotiating a way across the buttress which saved some height. By 05.10 hours it was getting dimly lighter and our walk home passed through several Wren territories with singing birds. George went to bed, I administered further tablets to a patient, did some reading, listened to the 1812 Overture, and had an early breakfast.

The halo around the moon at 03.00 hours signifying alto stratus, and suggesting a depression, proved positive, as by 07.15 it was raining hard with an increase in wind, so I sent off three mets. for different hours during the night to Benbecula, to inform them of the trough. Ration work during the day.

April 25

Rations all morning. Will Warner the OC suggested we went a walk and chose the Cambir (overlooking the Isle of Soay) as a destination and I thought going via Carn Mor would be of interest.

We set off at 13.45 hours and got to Am Blaid in good time, onto Mullach Sgar, and then to the Lover's stone, going below it, down the Gully and around the buttress, and picking our way across the slope we reached its far distant end, from where we were able to look down long green slopes and across to Soay. We were now searching for fresh paths on these slopes and came across sheep quite bewildered by our appearance, having not seen man for many months, We got as far as Geo na Lashulaich (the Firey Eyed Bay) when one of the slopes was too much for Will and he felt dizzy. I went on for a few yards and saw an unfavourable climb above the slopes and we consulted Prudence and went back the same way. It was good to have him there because I would never have ventured the final 150 yards alone. Having got back onto Carn Mor we took the route that George found the other night, and Will was by then glad of chances to rest. Once we had passed under Claigean Mor and found the old bank we walked down the road, getting back at 18.00 hours.

Q. Dedman took me to a newborn lamb behind the Manse that appeared to have picked up a second mother. After supper I took a quiet walk around the village.

April 26

Sunday. After breakfast spent some time listening to my usual Sunday morning programmes and at the same time sewed some fine elastic into the neck of my Fair Isle sweater knitted, lengthened and washed by Mary Stout of Busta in 1955. Overnight the wind had gone round to NNE, which explains why I needed to close my window during the night. After lunch went up to Am Blaid and beyond with George Mac, and we went very slowly along the path that runs under the steep slope on the SW side of Gleann Mor, finding Fulmars prospecting the rock face (inland).

This may be the first inland record but some years later in Svalbard, and possibly earlier in Iceland I recorded pairs nesting a quarter of a mile inland up valleys which may have given the young a better uplift when the did set off for the sea alone.

We continued further on to the Cambir (693ft, a slope of dwarf maritime sward) and on reaching Geo na Stacan we examined the terrain for possible paths, deciding it was possible to go right and not left. The lambs were showing great activity and seemingly larger than those in the village. Turning back we went down to Sgeir na Caraidh. Having walked around the Amazon's House in the depth of this glen, we walked back up the back slope of this gloomy north facing glen, over its containing bank, onto Mullach Sgar, and left handed to the village via the diesel dump.

April 27

I wrote an article for the RAMC Journal and did two walks around the village. A day with passing showers of rain water: we have run out of beer.

April 28

Having put aside all Ration work until the end of the week I was able to look at George's bird and sheep notes made during my absence. Fitted in a village walk and one to the Gap.

April 29

The weather records taken at the end of March were set out and an analysis started. While doing this a narrow deep trough passed over, taking about four hours. Very impressive. Another Bird Report went off to Ken Williamson (*more work for the Russian code breakers*).

April 30

At last I got an answer today to my query about the egg issue. Even via RT it has taken six days. A second day of dentistry today, both requiring repairs to improve the looks. They are all warned that the work is temporary and may need later army dental work or in civvy street. The work on one was so great that a nerve block was needed (*fortunately anatomy was my speciality!*). A messing meeting during the morning. There were few complaints (*when George did leave, he took a job as chef at the Choir School at Christ Church College Oxford*).

May 1

'Summer is icumin in lardly sing cuckoo.' No Cuckoo, and if it is summer, it came at 07.30 BST with the rattle of hail on the roof, and through the window. When I went down to breakfast the guilty cloud was across the bay dragging its fleecy feet behind it, as if becoming tardy on its course. During the morning I started calculating the rations for the issue tomorrow, when we are expecting an LCT bringing Dr Morton Boyd and five other civilians. There will be much stuff to be off and on loaded so she may well have to be here over two tides. After lunch Sgt. Murphy my Nursing Officer 2 and I got a lift up the road to Am Blaid, from where we went onto Carn Mor, past the Lover's Stone where we both posed as potential suitors. There were a pair of Puffin on land, and that 'small step' with each other's presence, gave them the courage to survey the world, and then turn round and dig, ignoring us.

Murphy had travelled the world with the Corps as a regular, and never thrived when he left the army: bereft of the army as a father, but with a mother he was devoted to near Glasgow.

The LCT leaves at 15.00 hours tomorrow.

May 2

Rations finished in good time. The wind got up and put an end to the boat sailing. Lazy afternoon but did a medium walk.

May 3

Sunday. A northerly wind around Oiseval and Dun gave a calm bay and prospect of excitement outside, but no gale where we were. It was agreed that we should send a landing party to the Island of Dun across the bay. The intention was to take eight in the dory, with the seaman and one other to take her back to the pier, landing six. We got off and back again singly over the bow, each one of us experiencing something different personally, and witnessing and helping five others. The flat rock we landed on was a 30 degree smooth slope extending at least one third the length of the island on the bay side and stopping higher up at a tussocky low cliff about 30ft high. The island was ungrazed, heavily tunnelled, and 576ft at its highest. The seaman decided go slowly up to the slope with bow on, wait for a wave to do a final heave, accept that the bow would smack down onto the rock (there were no points sticking up), hope that a jump and a push would get us out before a bigger wave, enabling the person to get a few feet higher. The landing slope was slimy and the plumber went first, and falling with feet just in the water, but standing firm when the wave retreated, he then slipped and we pulled him half back in to re-launch him after the next wave. Cpl. Denham then followed with a bow rope which was lost, so they threw the stern rope. Two waves then came at us head high and threw the bow upward onto the shelf. The next chap got nerves, so the one behind got past him and grabbed the now taut bow line with Denham at the top end and the plumber helping at the boat awash at every wave. My turn next. I remember a moderate wave taking us to within 3ft and making a jump and either not arriving or turning back once there, for my left hand was still on the gunwale, and as she was dragged out so did I follow. Next wave and I was there, a prostate body clutching to slime no longer than my own hair and vainly reaching for the rope. Before the next wave came I had got it and turned to watch Gunner Wathall in similar plight. We then fixed a permanent rope up, and found Bombardier Harris had dodged up unaided. He is someone who has had more experiences with skirmishes than most – and how to get out of them!

Between 14.45 hours and 17.00 hours I walked the full length of the island. There was evidence of ancient human use all the way along to the Shag colony at the south end. A great amount of valuable information gathered including the first clues to Puffin chick starvation. Will Warner was in the boat to get us off. One by one we got back to the boat. My own exit consisted of a bottom slide down the rope, the sight of a large wave about to lift the boat high and smack it down somewhere, the instinctive turn onto my front, with one foot dug in and one hand on a seaweedy patch, and another around someone's boot. My eyes closed as the sea washed up my front as far as my shoulders. The wave withdrew and I remained, but not for long; for the next wave, I dived for the open boat and was hauled further in by a number of strong arms.

May 4

I was fairly stiff this morning, but not bruised. I rose for breakfast at 07.30 hours and was relieved to see the LCT stranded well up on the beach, which would make unloading easier, and the loading of empty diesel drums safer. We breakfasted and then I started on the Ration books, soon having to hand over to Sgt. Murphy when I was interrupted by Capt. Bennet the Scot. Co. cipher expert, who had come across to teach the OC and myself how to use the One-Time letter pad codes. Next I had to see the Nature Conservancy party consisting of Morton Boyd, H.B. Carter from the Animal Breeding Research Dept. at Edinburgh, John Doney a geneticist from a Hill Farming Unit and Derek Ratcliff a well known botanist with the NC, who had all spent the night on the boat. Also with them was Murdo McDonald, a Coxwain from Tiree.

We had a large party for lunch and it included the No. 1 of the boat. The Staff Sgt. ACC for Scot. Co. had a long chat with me, and with many of the crew from the LCT coming over for the evening film, it was a fun day. All invitees had a smooth return to the now floating ship which was alight with lamps as if she was on the Riviera.

May 5

She slid out of the bay at 09.15 hours. I then set up a barograph which the Met. had sent at the request of the NC. Ration theory in the morning and Murphy did some practical flour carrying in the afternoon. After, I walked to the Gap and on to the talus slopes of Ard Uachdarachd; Puffins were sweeping their circular repetitive flights around me, and those up on the rocks peered and gaped at the intruder. Up on to Conachair top and across the col to Mullach Mor where Capt. Bill Ellis and his team worked at the VHF and spoke to his Major at the Range Head. Started home at 17.30 hours. Film in the evening. The NC lads had the help of a Scammel to get their boat down.

May 6

Did the Met. and then took Morton on the mice catching line. The sheep men examined, weighed, and jugular venepunctured last night's catch which had been penned up in the first house as yesterday (*the jugular vein in the sheep, at least a centimetre in diameter, lies outside the deep fascia of the neck 'contra to that of humans'. It does not lose too much heat in the wind because the wool and hair are thicker around the neck. The sheep in Patagonia, another windy habitat, have ruffs to protect these veins*).

After lunch I cut four heads of hair. I went catching sheep in the late evening with the sheep men.

May 7

Of late I have had less time for getting around because of more paperwork. The wind was up this morning; the same wind that had Morton's team up with myself at 04.30 hours to pull in their boat off its moorings. As a reciprocal gesture to him I filled one of his teeth today. A film in the evening, a misty rain at 21.00 hours, a deluge at 23.00 hours, the new barograph gave its first flick upwards, the wind veered and weakened: the cold front was through.

May 8

After breakfast I worked on the Rations to be issued tomorrow, then went to watch them processing the sheep caught last night, then held a messing meeting at 10.30 hours. After lunch six of us met in the Factor's House and gave ourselves areas to count the sheep. The important thing was that we counted in areas as delineated for a previous count. Knowing the island now better than any others, I am sure that many will be missed around the sea facing slopes, but constancy of method is vital, and then mistakes in method will still show acceptable comparisons. We had a lift up to Am Blaid at 14.30 hours and all went up to our respective areas getting back at 17.15 hours. The LCT bringing the 'Swans' has left.

May 9

When I awoke the LCT had been in the bay for a few hours, but had no intention of beaching until later in the morning at half tide. The sky was devoid of all cloud, and the May sun, rather more sure of itself, hung over the bay soaking the greener hills in light and warmth. I rearranged my room so that Bill Ellis could come in tonight. A lad with a fever needed attention, and I started on the Rations, and went on to read more of my letters before going up to change for supper. By the time I took my well earned village walk it had clouded over and was preparing to rain. Tomorrow the *S.S. Meteor*, an NTS cruise, arrives during the evening, just having left Foula. We have been given a passenger list to peruse.

May 10

The warm wind was most noticeable when I emerged this morning and seemed southerly in direction. Its source seems to be the mainland where it was so hot yesterday that 'it heated the heart and the head'. Here it lifted the soul to greater achievement, and with the *S.S. Meteor* due this evening there was some volatility. Being a Sunday it was a free day but I had too much to do to spend it outside. However a possible lift up to Am Blaid appeared and I took it and sat under the bank/wall around the top of the North Glen/Gleann Mor, the warm wind caressing the still yellow grass over which the lambs pranced and where their more placid mothers grazed, oblivious to their infantile elasticity. Derek Ratcliff took me over to Ruaival to see the Raven's nest, holding my arm as I leant over the cliff to photograph the nest.

Derek was a fine botanist, probably always associated with montane flora. During these studies he accumulated knowledge on Peregrine Falcon and Raven, writing a book on each was the mentor of the theory that it was insecticides that were thinning the eggshells of the birds and causing 'smashed eggs'. His work on the NVC showing that plants form complexes or associations was his most important contribution to plant ecology. He was an intense man, well suited to the work he did, and could produce more sense in a week without communication than a talkative idea swapping scientist would produce in a month.

My return journey took me a few faltering steps under the nest and then back to the village a direct way. The bay was fairly calm but came up with a SE wind later, which whipped up the sea, but did not last long, for serenity returned. I did some sewing and continually peeped out to see if our visitor had arrived.

Chapter Eight

....

Soay Ewe Casting

S.S. *Meteor* Arrives

At about 21.15 hours she came around Oiseval, flat funnelled, rather tubby, grey to white hulled and rather majestic. Slowly she slid into the bay nearer than the *Mull* would dare to enter. People lined the deck rails just as earlier in the day men had lined the bridge of the destroyer *H.M.S. Agincourt* when she had a quick glimpse at us.

Soon the long boat, a white solid tender boat, was swung over the side and lowered. Lord Polesworth and Mr Robertson landed on our pontoon and Col. Cooper, Capt. Warner and myself being there to meet them. The arrangements for next day were discussed and we were told that Ken Williamson hoped to land on Dun that evening.

Morton, Murdo and myself and a few of the lads went out in the Fulmar to watch them, but had little hope that they would succeed, for the swell was a little too much. The outcome was that they got Bob Hilcoat on and could not get him off, the boat getting into a periodic swing which got wider and longer with her screw coming right out of the water. Wisely they retreated and I shouted to Ken that they would be better going to Carn Mor. They got to the pier before us and Ken gave the welcome to me on our return. Geoffrey Boswell arrived with his recording equipment from the BBC and so also did Dr Joe Eggeling from Edinburgh NC. All came up to the Mess and a little *aqua vitae* was taken. I had met Geoffrey on Skokholm, and Ken was my Code bird contact. We then formed the Carn Mor party and I changed into less respectable attire and got bird rings, chocolate, four tins of beer and a torch. Four of us took a lift to Am Blaid and splitting the heavy equipment headed for Carn Mor along the wall, then, taking the diagonal across the slope were soon sliding down the four hundred foot high gulley with the comforting buttress on our right.

May 11

We must have rounded the buttress around midnight, Geoff doing the last few feet in a rather spectacular manner head first. Distorted slabs loomed up in the dark and we moved a further 50ft down where we could hear Manxies calling loudly, with 'swooshing' and the occasional 'plomp' of a landing bird which would soon be scrambling down into the tunnelled boulder mass, their deep calls alone betraying their presence.

We tried to find the double cleit but I made an error and we arrived at a 20ft boulder at what could be called the centre but with all the noise under and around it resembled Piccadilly without its lights. Joe Eggeling had found the cleits and was flashing his torch. We took off our loads and Geoffrey, feeling the effects of the climb, announced his intention to communicate with 'Somnus'. Where should he go? Ken abruptly said that if the cleits were good enough for St Kildans they were good enough for him; so bow first he slowly rotated himself into the entrance and lowered himself onto a comfy set of boulders. Joe went into the other cleit, Ken sat on his haunches and took it all in, and I moved higher up where the Shearwaters were denser. Now the Leach's Petrels were calling. The star gazing Shearwaters were easily picked up and their nipping quite as annoying as the Welsh ones. Several were ringed and after an hour I rejoined Ken and we went on further looking for more Leach's Petrels, eventually coming out on the ridge at the end of the Mor where there was more grass and a great number of fluttering birds.

It was nearer 02.45 hours when we returned. We found fewer swooping birds and more underground. Geoffrey emerged from his cleit, sliding around on leather soled shoes. We re-found Ken and discussed what he was going to talk about on the recording. An account of our activities was given and as dawn crept up Shearwaters shot like shells over our heads as they started on a few days feeding trip. It was 04.30 hours. Wrens were waking, their bodies shimmering in vocal ecstasy with head held high, chests thrown forward, and drooping wings. It was noticeable that each bird awaited its turn. Geoff and I also rotated roles with the equipment. Joe had now awoken. We took the newly discovered way off the talus discovered by George Mac, and met up by the Lover's stone, getting back to base direct or indirectly as we chose. A pink glimmer in the east had fused sea and sky. I put Ken and Geoffrey to bed in the MI room and the two heaps of blankets moved with gentle breathing by 06.30 hours. I did a Met. report, had a bath, and ironed my trousers. Breakfast for those awake at 08.00 hours and at 08.45 people were seen coming off the boat.

The first boat consisted of elderly female arthritics who we hoisted out and briskly pulled up the steps where they assembled with thanks for deliverance, and were guided up the slipway onto the top and herded into a flock. Some with more ability broke loose and wisely headed for the village.

The second load arrived with an elderly lady who, freely admitting she was no fairy, put her foot through one inch planking on the deck of the pontoon, a feat never before accomplished, even during the winter off loading of the *Mull*. The flock that had landed was growing. Voices were raised. Bright red hats, pink trousers and black satin garments resembling 'shorty nighties' raised a clamour from the Herring Gulls on Oiseval. Two lorries were starting to load the non walkers for a lift to the top. The village sheep looked on with evasive bewilderment as the bridgehead expanded into an invasion.

Ken was now present, his hair a little shaggier than usual. At half past nine half had been conveyed to the top, but already the leaders were in retreat. An Armenian lady had found herself unable to walk around on Mullach Mor and had radioed down for help. Ten minutes later she emerged from the back of a Land Rover well satisfied with St Kilda.

Mullach Mor had started to glint in the sun, and clouds, soft and thin drifted over her bare shoulder, while on her head a collection of visitors had gathered, second only to those seen on the East Bank at Cley, Norfolk, were a Dodo to have been seen. For the ladies, headgear alone could have covered all possible fashions from 966AD to 1966, except for the absence of flowers, pheasant feathers and ostrich plumes. The gentlemen's rig out varied from John Betjeman's trilby, mackintosh and carrier bag, to the gentleman from Kentucky who had designed a head gear to raise his immunity to the constant chatter of his 'admirable' wife.

I moved over to a group looking down onto Gleann Mor: three ladies, two tweedy gents and John Betjeman, and discussed the significance of the Amazon's House. I was on the verge of explaining my lesbian theory when Ken came up and we both encouraged people to go to points of their choice and gave them guidance. Some headed back to the lunch time boat. Geoffrey, our BBC man was up and about with a large parabolic reflector in the meadows. My legs were a little heavy but lunch soon revived them, and after, Morton and the two sheep scientists set off for Boreray with Murdo.

I organised tea for 16.00 hours and quickly went around the village finding one lost woman who I took around Tobar Childa. Gradually the wanderers assembled in the Recreation Room for a buffet tea. Officers who had only been here a few days were embarrassed to be plied with questions on the winter, the flowers, the mighty cliffs, the habitations and its previous inhabitants. I helped them out if they were failing. The cooks had done a good job and cakes were eagerly engulfed, and an occasional pair of youthful legs 'swallowed' by the lads. At 17.15 hours I took a small party to see some Snow Buntings in the village, and then went back to the Factor's House to change into my Patrols for dinner on board (*the RAMC being historically a mounted Regiment had a smart dark tight uniform suitable for riding in, as on patrol*). Our visit was preceded by a cocktail party in the mess. A lady who had been guided by me during the day regarded my conversion as worth a fit of giggles when she saw me outside the MI Room being photographed by my staff. I am at least adaptable! My entry into the Mess was belated and I had two sherries in five minutes to catch up. Henry Douglas Home, a good naturalist asked me about the breeding cycle of the Fulmar. He lives at Old Grenfrew, Berwickshire and had his daughter Fiona with him, so free speech on the endocrine situation in the Petrel was limited. John Betjeman was looking tired and a lady from Chelsea was with him. BBC Geoffrey then entered and took me off to do my recording on the sex life of the Soay sheep with special reference to their nuptial chases. It was hurried and done in a cleit to reduce the wind effect. Patrols were not designed for sitting in cleits. However I wish he had given me more time to prepare it. I was told later that when he played it to the Natural History Unit on his return, it was the first time they had laughed on a Monday morning. Even as we finished the boat was leaving and we had to call it back. They were glad to have us on board and wined and dined us in good style with the other ranks messing down below 'meeting' the crew of <u>both</u> sexes. They thought highly of the Scandinavian crew, all of whom cheered us as we left after we had cheered them (*the fuller account is in my original books. Shall we leave it at that!*).

For myself the main lasting important memory was meeting John Betjeman for a long table talk at dinner about the Amazon's House, and the possibility that the name is not of local origin but was ascribed to the people living there by learned visitors who had read of the Amazons abroad, and related them to the verbal history heard here. He said that the Celts were a matriarchal society and to my comment that that could be close to lesbianism, he nodded. There is no doubt that the bank/wall was designed to keep people in the glen and not to be a defensive mechanism to keep the village bay inhabitants out. It is a kind of punishing isolation area offering a desolate location, perhaps from a large area in the region.

I have been a long time without bed or sleep and it seems that my student days with long spells in residence on duty all the time has held me in good stead.

May 12

Morning work in the MI Room but many took the morning off. After lunch Morton, Derek and myself went over to Dun, landing on the steep good rock to the right of the cleft. The slope is NE facing but away from the wind it was warm. Puffins circled, all anti-clockwise as we climbed over the soft yielding turf in order to climb Bioda Mor, just over 500ft high. There was a continuous hum from these several thousand birds, whose presence necessitated an extra camera 'stop' with the dimmed light. The smell of the Puffins and Petrels was as fragrant to me as the blossoms in the orchards of Worcestershire; no bees here and no Puffins there. From the top the Fulmar fishing in the bay with its orange colour standing out against the blue sea was the only other human activity. Away to the left Mullach Bi was smoking like a chimney, and to the right a thick layer of orographic cloud with cumuliform tops was drifting towards Conachair, throwing some of the village areas into shade. Having flirted with Conachair the flimsy vanished as wisps over its eastern cliffs, just leaving the top with a veiled crown.

   At 16.30 hours we all met at the landing place and departed with great ease: how different to the last departure which was like dropping from a prancing horse into a canoe. I sketched my proposed painting of Dun in the evening.

May 13

The day was set calm, but low cloud hung across the hills. We decided to try and land on Stac an Armin, the 627ft high Stac in the Boreray group of islands which had never been landed on without a native guide and never by any one since 1932, the year of my birth. This tall white topped stack, the further of the two, standing defiant to gales and seas for years, each summer receives its crowds of Gannets, Fulmars, Razorbills, and Puffins, and last winter stood nose in the air, snooty in its secure aloofness; scornful of its sister Hirta with her uninvited guests treading and driving over her. Today we hoped to remove that smirk from its face, for although it shows an almost vertical face to Hirta; to Boreray and the Flannans it is more genteel.

We left about 09.30 hours and were soon leaving Oiseval behind us. The sea was calm and without any wind and the Fulmars were having to fly and not glide. At 10.00 hours I gave the first Aero report of the day to Benbecula on a small portable wireless via our signals centre on Hirta. Fifteen minutes later we were passing Stac Li, a few thousand Gannets leaving their lofty perch to fly over us were able to defecate to their bowels' content. There were over 20,000 pairs on these three rocks and we had 5,000 birds bombing us. To our right was Boreray, with a few green verdant slopes on which could be seen some of the flock of 450 Black faced sheep. Ahead was our goal and between Stac Li and Boreray in the 150 yard wide passage was a single sharp crag startlingly black in the white seas that broke over it.

We steered between this and a possible landing place, but a look soon told us that the swell was too much, so rounding the corner to the most sheltered eastern side we were in calm water and able at our leisure to pick a new landing place. Two men were at the oars to steady her in. The landing place was a ten foot high vertical rock face with a little short seaweed on and no visible footholds. The boat was rising and falling four to five feet but there was no sea breaking or even showing white. Morton took the first chance, and seemed to pull himself up, though I never saw what he jumped onto, and only heard discouraging remarks while he looked down on us. My turn next and I saw a flat triangular protuberance about five inches high which could be as near as a foot from extended arms at the top of the swell. I jumped at this and hung there as the boat dropped away beneath me, leaving my feet dangling, perhaps waiting for the boat to come up to meet them. I cannot recall any such meeting but holding the hand hold with my left hand now close to my left shoulder, I felt up with my right and found something and pulled up beside Morton, turning around while sitting there to guide Derek Ratcliffe onto the holds I used. John Doney who the other day did get on to Boreray, did not try it. The boat drew away.

We stood where no man had trod for 27 years and set off to find the old fowling track. We went lower and slid around a steep but not vertical rock face on our backs in order to get up onto a wide ledge where we turned right and slowly gained height until we were under the tussocky green slopes on the east side, with the boat marking time far below us and Gannets wheeling over their heads. My camera was continually at work from when we found the ruins of the old bothy. Morton and Derek were keen to get to the top but we were limited to an hour, and though it would mean missing personal contact with the Gannets at the top, I could not have changed film also, and get close to the artefacts and birds where I now was. When two thirds of the way up I slowly walked down, photographing on the way. Morton and Derek came up behind me when I was 50ft above our contact point. The wind was just starting to freshen. Derek (the only non swimmer) was first to jump (it was not possible to see the boat) but he was 'encouraged'; I followed with Faith though both of us needed to find the hooked rock that helped us earlier.

Morton sent wireless messages to Hirta to tell them that we had got on and off safely, and this triggered messages to *S.S. Meteor* and the *Scotsman*, and enabled a Shackleton to fly to the group to photograph the bird numbers as we were there.

On reaching the bay I was rather exhausted and after a late lunch slept deeply in the chair for half an hour. In the evening we circumnavigated Hirta through Soay Sound and checked on the place they intended to land at tomorrow.

May 14

Morton got to Soay, and I was in the MI room during the day, and walked to the Gap in the evening. No sheep in the cleits tonight so we did not catch any.

May 15

The morning Messing meeting was delayed till after lunch. By late evening there was a fog selectively at mid height over Dun and Ruaival.

May 16

The phenomenon of the fog persisted, and after lunch in my walk along Glacan Conachair with John Doney, I was able to see it just as Heathcote had drawn it in his book. We went up to the Gap and at the cliff edge were above the swirling mist he described. This was about 400ft deep with a clear top which lay like cotton wool. The Boreray group appeared like a sick child sitting in bed with cotton wool packed in tight around it. We had a small party for Derek, John and Nick in the Mess to mark their departure tomorrow.

May 17

Sunday. The LCT arrived just after midnight but was going to be unable to beach until 18.00 hours today. However at

09.00 hours we put out the dory, and started bringing off the newcomers which included Graham, another sheep chap, and another Signals man to see Capt. Ellis re. the VHF link. In the morning John and I took Graham over to see the Amazon's House in Gleann Mor. After lunch I wrote my migration report for Ken, and wrote a quick letter home and two business letters. After tea offloading took place while the water washed around her bow over the sand. I escorted those departing to the boat and went back to have a drink with the Skipper, Ian Perridin, in the Mess, and then dealt with two minor injuries. Ian left at 22.00 hours and we both shipped onto the ramp going in for coffee with our previous mess mates. I rowed the dory to the pier with the LCT seaman and he took it back alone.

May 18

Whit Monday and officially a day of rest. My first contact with the outside air was 07.30 hours when I helped the lad with soft tissue injuries incurred during the off loading, back onto the boat. He had been sleeping in the MI room at night. The boat left soon after with white plumes of water surging around her bows. From mid morning I did an extensive walk of the village, and after lunch went up to the Gap, with the hot sun beating on my back, I sat on my usual perch for a short time, then crossed over to Oiseval, reaching the top at 16.00 hours. The main chain of the Hebridean Islands swung low across the horizon with rather more cloud than we had, but soon we had a small dose ourselves. I walked down to the lower path and then on to the camp.

The grass is now growing strongly and even too fast for ewes that were hungry, and lambs who could always take a nutritional maternal short cut. In places the 'heather' showed that it too can catch an eye that looks for spring. The tups that grazed these withered shrubs in the winter now ignored them. Their old fleeces hang waiting to be cast, and short trim hair growth shows underneath.

The Soay hair and some wool has a short brittle section where it easily breaks and can be cleanly removed with the side of the hand. This could be a genetic tendency or stress or a combination of each, occurring at the growth point and showing later.

The ewes are more placid and better bonded to their lambs, but are having to grow a new fleece and provide milk at the same time.

Small fronds of bracken started to uncurl three days ago, and primroses and violets have been in flower four weeks. A purple orchid and a lousewort also recorded. Fulmar Petrels laid some first eggs a week ago. The Resurrection is here; silently and steadily in the last week it has come to all, though all may not yet have risen.

May 19

I lay in the hot sun at Tobar Childa for half an hour in the morning to rest from the laborious business of decoding the weather reports for April, entering them onto F3203 (1955). In the afternoon I took Graham Gunn around the known sheep skeletons. After tea I started on my painting of Dun, finishing it at 18.30 hours. I have been missing most of the films on fine summer evenings, but tonight refrained from missing June Halliday and Kim Novak. With hotter days the sheep seem to have reversed their cleit resting period from night to day.

Cleit creeping is both an art and a science, for though unknown in other cultures it has made swift progress here in the Hirtensiocene period. Parties of three or four, 'stealthily on footsteps creeping' will approach a cleit into the wind and block the entrance with their body turned back on to them.

The sheep hurl themselves at one's back (it is best to kneel) and by grabbing a pair of horns one can use the captive animal to further block the entrance, eventually throwing him and tying two legs together for better control. Lambs usually have to have both sets of legs tied.

They then need to be cared for in the house ready for measuring and marking the next day so have to be carried there, each bearing method having 'pros and cons'. The most unpleasant con is the ejection of urine down the collar when slung on the neck with a firm grip on a pair of legs each side. The 'babe in arms approach' presents the same problem in a different direction. The cleit creeper has two vocal responses given with an extended neck, the first a muffled shout poorly heard, and the second casts doubt on the parentage of the sheep which is a little unfair because so few of the animals have any genealogical knowledge and take such remarks very seriously. After penning them in the first house the cleit creepers retire to bed.

May 20

At 10.25 hours I walked from the camp to Tobar Childa and then up onto the col between Conachair and Mullach Mor and with a left turn reached Marconi Radar set at just after 11.00 hours. Glen Bay looked quiet and even tempting, with Fulmars and seals. I called in to see Bill and his lads working on the VHF at Marconi and then walked along the Glen side of the road to Mullach Sgar and onto Ruaival overlooking Dun and back along the cliff edge to the village where I told Morton about the Quail. I walked the village after lunch and did a little 'Fulmar watching'. The Royal Fleet Auxiliary vessel has called and refuelled the buoys, moving one to a more convenient position. The Skipper landed and was most co-operative.

May 21

'Open O fathomless pit with thy terrors'; Bach's St Matthew's Passion. This morning's work: repair of a tooth, excision of a sebaceous cyst, and work on the cess pit.

The wind dropped considerably during the morning and at lunch time Morton suggested a second trip to Boreray. We had to wait for the tide to rise as the boat was lying beyond a great heap of *Laminaria*. We pulled her in at 14.30 hours and Morton, coxswain Murdo, Graham Gunn, Robin Ward a TA para. sapper, a rare 'breed', Gnr. Wathal, Cpl. Pare and myself, together with Compo rations, spare engine, fresh water and numerous other nautical and scientific gadgets on loaded we started out of the bay.

The sun was hot but there was a suspicion of high cloud to the east. There was enough breeze to cool the face and a slight choppy sea in the tidal race off Oiseval. Gliding Fulmars and diving Puffins were always there. The Gannets joined us as we approached the stacs. Ahead the seas were breaking around Gob Scapanish, and as we rounded it our landing place came into view, tucked inside Coirneag, just on the left of the innermost part.

There was a gentle swell, the tide being at half flow, but rather quieter against the landing place than 20 yards further out, where the sea 'boiled' as if churned by August mackerel. Gently the bow of the boat was edged up to the rock, Morton crouching in the bow, and as she touched he leapt onto the slippery but wide ledge. On the same rise I followed, and Robin and Graham were soon also ashore. The next step was an eight foot perpendicular rock face with a high foothold and a hand high grip near the top, a climb that was easier enough if a little pushing on the posterior was given underneath. Being the last person I had no such aid, but Robin kindly lowered a foot for me to grab and we were then all on a large flat rock, sloping upwards at about 30 degrees, up which we all walked in primitive Neanderthal style. Then we made our way without gain or loss of height, self taking up the rear, and then down a 20ft slope and round the corner to see the flat slabs we needed to cross to get to a position to climb the grassy slopes to Cleitan Mcphaiden. Morton announced twice that he knew this place like the back of his hand (*he wrote in my diary at this point "not hand – head! JMB"*) then led the way up a rock with Robin following. Robin was half way up when Morton realised that his hand must have changed and announced an immediate withdrawal. Robin was vexed and both came down and we all re-gathered on the slab. From here we went down to a cliff equal in height to the one Robin had just half climbed and found ourselves on the slabs we wanted.

Rarely has a single step been anticipated with greater gloom, partly because Morton had presented it to so many as the biggest hindrance to advancement on Boreray beyond the lower part of the cliff. Its appearance in no way fell short of my expectations. A chasm four foot across, a hundred foot deep, and extending 50 yards from the water's edge into the island lay between us and further progress. The slab surface both sides were at 40 degrees and there were no footholds, so what would have been a large step were it a foot deep, was through its greater depth and angled take off and landing, very much worse. Directly below the water in a calm manner surged and slopped, and my stomach reacted in sympathy as a deep nausea.

Morton crossed. I awaited next and Graham and Robin sat behind me. I looked across and down, down and across, shifting from one foot to another. Morton stands and records my plight on film. A few words were said: he stands to catch me yet not to stop me. A final look to the antipodes and then

I jumped. Two across and two behind. Graham made it but Robin declined.

The grass approach to the summit of 1245ft was a dry slog and until I got my second wind there seemed little hope of reaching it; and if I got there at 16.50 hours, that would leave me ten minutes to get down. It was 16.30 hours. The Blackface sheep, long haired and log horned, departed in thin lines ahead of me, decidedly fleeter of foot and looking cool in spite of their thick fleeces.

I walked up towards Tigh Stallar. Stac Li was below me, its ledges crammed white with Gannets, but they were far away as were the birds on Boreray, and not suitable for photography. At 16.50 I was still 200ft from the top, and had to turn and alternately run and walk down the grassy slope thinking it was the correct one. It was not, but I did find Robin on his haunches watching seals. The chasm was still there, and I was the wrong side of it. Morton and Graham turned up ten minutes later and as I perused the problem peering into the dark, a seal blew a resonant snort below me. I was reminded of the Roman Catholic Father who, eating seal on a Friday because it was a fish, was admonished by an Episcopalian, who said it could not be a fish for he had heard seals breaking wind backwards.

We all crossed and twisted our way back along the ledges, Robin with twin holes in his shorts from sitting. Our landing ledge was awash during the wave surge and we had to time our drop accordingly, but once down it was a matter of awaiting the right moment and springing into the boat, which up to now had been marking time fifty yards out. Three cheers for the crew and we continued our circumnavigation of the group, noting some other features. A calm journey back and we went into the bay at 18.50 hours, and took off for supper.

May 22

A small party went to Levenish today to fix up a reflector for the signallers. I had a Messing meeting, and then did the Met. and had cocoa. Then worked on tomorrow's Ration issue, and was rewarded with a few migrants in the village. During the hot afternoon, Robin Ward, our T.A. Para. Sapper set off two explosions down by the pier to clear some boulders away from the approach channel. It was effective, and also cleared the beach of Gulls.

I am reminded that when the RAF were first here some Spaniards arrived on the pier with guns threatening Wing Co. Cookson if he did not allow them to shoot. He said they had no small guns but had a big gun on the hill. He then telephoned the lads at the quarry and asked for a single blast of explosives when he ordered. Comforted by this promise he put more pressure on and then gave the word. The bang cleared Gulls and Spaniards fairly quickly.

Morton took the boat around to Glen Bay and I walked over the top to Gleann Mor. Gulls were now on eggs and Oystercatchers possibly so. I walked along to Gob na Airde, continuing along the ledge to the natural arch which outlined the view of Boreray, once one was inside it with the Guillemots, some nodding and others growling. The diagonal walk back up to the crossroads was slow but pleasant. My return was straight down ignoring the road.

May 23

Rations in the morning. Robin made more big bangs after lunch and then took his lads up to the top to do some concreting, where he was due to meet me. We then both went to Conachair summit around 16.45 hours and did a slow two hour walk around to Conachair via the village side to Ard Uachdarachd, the north east shoulder of the hill, climbing down to the cleit ledge, from where we made our way round the grass slopes to the loose talus, above Stac a Langa, and set off for Conachair top along the well trodden path. Back to the village at 18.30 hours. At 23.30 I left for Carn Mor with Robin and George.

May 24

Sunday. We returned from Carn Mor at 02.30 hours. I spent much time in the dark room producing prints of varying quality. The LCT is expected tomorrow morning.

May 25

I breakfasted at 08.30 hours and found the LCT in the bay and at 09.00 hours those intending to land were brought ashore in the dory. Capt. Douglas Upton had come to relieve Will as OC for two weeks and Lt. James Mackay arrived for a two week stay; Lieut. Nobby Hall has come to rearrange the setup of the Decca Radar, and Major Allday to hold a Court of enquiry.

My morning was as hectic as any boat day: acting as GPO boss, sorting, answering my and MO mail, washing sheets, retrieving rations and briefing officers arriving in the Mess. After lunch the boat was beached and Skipper Peter Jones and Lieut. Leach came ashore to replenish body fluids and we went over to them for coffee, returning for tea. After supper Graham Gunn, Morton and Will prepared to leave. Morton had made full use of his time with the boat. Robin had been good company, and Will will be back.

A small fishing vessel drew up in the bay, containing a small NTS party, and I spent some time helping them to get settled and getting their Rations, which had been sent on a previous LCT, out of the store.

I am a fair man and must copy out what final crack Robin had made at my diary before leaving. 'Unfortunately the record of St Kilda Minutes must here end. The diarist was last seen leading the three young ladies that had landed this evening from a fishing smack towards their camp site saying, "I'll show you to your tents", since then there has been only silence other than a remark in Latin, "Amasne odorem meum novum".'

May 26

The falsity of the above insinuation was established when in the little time I had today I found five men in the NTS party including Alex Warwick.

May 27

I took the NTS party around Oiseval on the high path coming out by the Gap. Jim was disadvantaged by leather soled boots and was not alone in respect shown for the slopes. I watched the party very carefully as I intended to take them to Carn Mor. I very rarely showed them where we were going first because it invariably worried them. The most important things were proper shoes and clothing and the need to do what they were told. We assembled at 23.30 hours.

May 28

The going was hard and dry. Little patches of mist flicked the hill tops. At 00.30 hours we met up with two who had gone ahead at the Lover's stone and took my prescribed route down, the twisting line of torches passing onto the talus and on to the cleit with the poles and nets in. We moved on, Petrels hit the net but we caught none. All handled Manx Shearwaters, some for the first time, and Alex came through the dark with what seemed to be a deep growling sea shanty, but what was an indignant Puffin, nipping and clawing as we handled him.

We packed around 03.00 hours. Most of the group were novices, appreciating brief stops, but they did well, returning the usual way, and at 04.00 hours I was listening to a Wren singing from the Factor's House chimney.

May 29

Awakened at 08.00 hours and rose at 08.30 hours. I removed a wart from the plumber's hand. The water situation is worrying and we have only had 19.0 mm so far in the month of May. Col. Cooper has been spoken to. A walk and a book read were fitted in.

May 30

Ration issue today. My proverbial shepherding walk produced a tapeworm discarded by a sheep which was 10ft long with an intact head.

What is a cleit? It is a stone building longer than it is broad, and about as broad as it is high, roofed with stone slabs over which a thick growth of turf grows. A door through which a sheep can comfortably walk is situated either at one end or the side, and the earthen floor of soil and compressed faeces is rarely wet, just damp, as the wind blows through it with a load of salt, which used to preserve the dead birds in such a manner that they dried up and retained their unusual flavour. The Trust members invited us to a party in one, with benches and candlelight, ferns around the entrance and a pile of beer cans at the far end. Have you ever walked into a cocktail party backwards in a crouching position, being given navigation directions from behind to avoid clashing with a naked flame? The alternative was to dive in; which could be taken as a deliberate dive at the drink. Alex's songs were followed by some spoof second sight games. The food was improvised but adequate and interesting, and somehow escaped the wax from dripping candles, though we did not. One guest took my advice as to whether, if he did accept the fact that he was going to be fixed in wax, should he choose for his legs to be bent or straight.

May 31

Sunday. The rain has come. 13.6 mm measured this morning but none between 9th and 28th. I started to paper maché my island model. In the finer PM I took the group up Conachair via the Gap. The Oystercatcher nest by the store has one young.

June 1

The carpenter was competing with silence in the MI Room. After lunch I returned to the Ration Books, and before tea walked the village. After tea I cut my own hair to mark the start of the Scottish summer. In the evening the Trust party came down and played the lads at snooker, darts, billiards and table tennis, and put me in the Trust table tennis team.

June 2

A hard blow during the night after a sudden drop in ppp (atmos. pressure) overnight but was not quite at gale force anytime during the morning. However the sea was stirring after a long period of welcome torpidity. With the rain of two days ago after a drought the grass in the wetter areas are greener. The sheep, with loose hanging fleeces, are very tempting as carriers of potential tweed, but I have only caught two in the open by stalking, usually failing in the final tackle, with 'me' on the grass and the sheep away and safe. My trap line gave me a mouse to show the NTS party, and one dared to handle it. Films still take place weekly, but I missed tonight's in favour of trouser repairing. Perhaps this shows I am missing surgery.

June 3

After break I went with Doug and Jim up in a lorry to Am Blaid, from where we went to the Decca and trekked down to the reflective beacon to see how hard it is likely to be to shield or remove it, to confirm its exact position on the radar screen. I went up for a quick look but the wind was too strong for any gymnastics. We went left handed via the beach to the camp and I did my village walk after. The sea was racing high today and it was not anticipated that the boat would come to bring a relief party for the NTS.

Today a Compo. biscuit tin, suitably weighted, and with inflated polythene bags inside containing letters, was sent off from Point of Col. Its white flag swung with the pendulum motion of the mail boat, exposing the red letters St Kilda Mail, on the side.

This was later found by John MacArthur, Sandwick, Doune Carloway, Lewis on June 14th 1959 when he was getting in his lobster creels.

June 4

I got up at 03.45 hours and started on a Wren count of the village area. The known local ones and others who were guarding their discreet territories with strong song (louder than the mainland 'race') were all marked and counted onto a map. Soon huge cumuliform clouds were turning pink from the morning sun which must have arisen over Boreray, hidden from me by the Gap. As I got back to bed at 05.00 hours our local wren sung at me from our chimney.

Three features adapt this species to a windy shrubless habitat as regards vocalisation. Firstly the absence of an alarm call in the absence of predators, secondly having a louder song, and thirdly singing from a prominent, well exposed site.

The main job of the morning was the removal of the top off the Radar Beacon. Jim, myself, Pt. Rhodes, and Cpl. Riley, Royal Signals, went along with a ladder and climbing belts. Riley managed well and the removal and re-erection of the top was carried out by noon. For some reason I was put in charge of this. Perhaps there is a vague medical connection. In the afternoon I photographed the Oystercatcher, with an odd set up of camera and iron bars, the whole procedure carried out blind.

After tea I went up to the Gap to look out for the seine vessel due from Tarbert. At 18.45 hours she came around Oiseval, plunging and twisting, with a clump of cold people on the deck, desperate for land. They were soon off and Irene Waterston told Alex Warwick that the boat intended to leave that night and not in the morning. The rowing boat left the trawler at 20.00 hours to pick up the passengers with their luggage.

June 5

Rhodes and I did the Rations early and got them finished in good time. After lunch I got a lift up to Marconi with the signals officer Bill Ellis, and then walked down onto Glacan

Conachair. Conachair cliff looked sinister but with the Fulmars almost flirting with it. Walking along the cliff edge I was half an hour later at Gob na Airde, and swinging left among mewing gulls towards the glen itself. I spent some time photographing the houses from different angles and with just the one fixed lens on my camera, my variation was limited. There were thin puffy clouds over the glen and thicker ones over Mullach Mor, casting fleeting shadows on the floor and over the south east side. I climbed to the left, contouring round to the beacon, where air, rushing up the tall green slopes, surrendered itself into cloud as if confused and beaten by its own headlong precipitous passage.

Much of today was spent preparing Met. reports for the LCT which is leaving the Long Island sometime today, and the evening was occupied worrying about her arrival, for she had ideas about beaching on the rising tide at 04.30 hours on my birthday tomorrow morning. This is bad enough anyhow, but a 16 ton Radar No. 4 Mark 7 had to come off and the swell in the bay was not pleasant. Thus it was that my Met. messages, though true to facts, were biased as to conclusion and did not encourage such escapades.

June 6

In vain we had pleaded that the sea was too much to permit a landing, but she would wait until <u>her</u> appreciation gave the answer, and at 03.15 hours she came in to see. As this kept us from our beds, to say the least we were a little touched. Even the Norwegian trawler had yet to commit herself to anchoring and had not got 'anchored' lights on. We fired two Very lights high into the air to persuade the LCT to listen to our RT signals but she failed to respond, came in, took a look at the beach, did an emergency turn around the trawler, and retreated to Glen Bay on the north side of the island. All this we could have foretold after supper, and now she was advising us that there was no safe anchorage in Village Bay and she was going around the corner. Bed at last and as the Factor's House Wren opened up at ten second intervals at 03.35 hours, my head sunk into my pillow.

When I did rise, low cloud and rain swept angrily across the sea and hills and persisted in doing so all the morning. At 13.00 hours blue patches appeared and the wind dropped. This was promising and as the tide flowed during the afternoon, there was promise of a quieter sea for the evening high tide at 19.30 hours. At 16.00 hours my Met. calculations were promising and once given to her she announced her intention to beach soon after 22.00 hours. The residual swell was due to a severe gale in south Rockall which had now moved across Ireland. Twenty minutes later she opened her doors, and choosing the right moment I was first on, but not without a waist high wetting. Pushing the ward room curtains aside revealed Captains Beauly and Earl, Dr David Jenkins and Col. Winfield. Skipper Peter Jones took me to see two patients he had, and when all was organised I waded off the boat.

It was raining hard, but under an oilskin I was dry, even though during the next hour we were seeing to the removal (or rather non removal) of the Mark 7 Radar and I was constantly in and out of the water. The Colonel came down and we discussed the situation in view of the large hole that had formed at the bottom of the ramp. I went on again with Rhodes and got the meat out of the fridge.

June 7

Sunday. At 01.30 hours the tide was at its lowest. It was now or never: now it was; for with an almost bereaved Colonel wringing his hands on the ramp lest it should stick or drown, the Mark 7 was slowly dragged off. At 03.00 hours the officers re-embarked to return to Benbecula, a technical signaller with them.

During the morning the first professional examination ever to have been held on St Kilda took place. Jim Mackay took it in the MI Room; the invigilator was the strict and stern Doc. He was sitting the Meeting Section of the Chartered Institute of Secretaries, and from 10.00 hours to 13.00 hours I sat reading my sister's birthday present from me on horse psychology, keeping a very open eye on Jim, who, his face weathered in honesty and mental labour, was busily writing. To be impartial he should be referred to as HEBRIDES 1. Horse psychology did not prove of great value in interpreting his mind.

The rations had to be done and the mail sorted. Jim had written to a philatelic magazine so that we were inundated with requests from Britain and America asking for letters to be sent with the St Kilda post mark on, in various forms. The slides of Stac an Armin have come back and encouraged me to do similar photography on the west cliffs under safer conditions. Jim and I included a walk down to Dun passage, using only one hand as the other protected my camera lens.

We crouched in the spray laden wind as angry seas threw themselves into the opening, bursting white with anguish; their efforts spoiled by rocks and cliffs. Their failure was our success, for the chance of a few photos was not wasted. I did a village walk in the evening while a film was being shown.

June 8

During the morning I cleaned up the Met. instruments to relieve them of salt. I slept for a short time after lunch while the rain pattered on the roof, and at 14.15 hours I left with Jim and David Jenkins and had to rally the pair after two sharp showers so as to continue over Mullach Bi to the neck of the Cambir via a cliff top route. On the return I noted Fulmars were now sitting on the inland cliffs at the top of the glen. One more storm and we were back at 18.15 hours.

June 9

Medical duties in the morning. I took David Jenkins up Conachair and he did some photography up there. We returned via the Gap. Irene Waterston came in for a drink and a chat.

June 10

At last the weather looks bright again after a slow rise in pressure during the last few days. Some mouse examinations this early morning and a drug check with Sgt. Larham. I went around the village with Alan Aitken (NTS) and David Jenkins (NC) and pointed out some topographical features I had found during the last few months. Jim worked in Calum Mor.

June 11

The first few minutes of the day were spent getting down the long grass slopes on the way to Carn Mor. I had walked up the road in twenty minutes while three female members of the NTS party followed behind in the Land Rover. The walk around the wall was rather funereal in speed but we took my approved short cut to the gully and were then able to fit body form to microtopography according to choice. It was 22.45 hours. Some shapes fitted no ground form but they managed without self control. We dumped our baggage at the first cleit and then moved over to a grassy area, later bringing the nets over and catching a few Shearwaters and Leach's Fork

Tailed Petrels. One of the latter we took back for photography in the morning.

Here follows in my diary a detailed description of a succession of underground chambers at three different levels each one entered via a tight hole between boulders from an adjoining chamber, no chamber big enough to hold more than three people. Shearwaters sat around singly or in pairs. Other smaller chambers would only admit an outstretched arm. There must have been 20 to 30 birds mostly at an arm's length from the next nest. The hole we first entered was 21ft from the final chamber floor and birds could be heard further along and down, the arrangement resembling a well spaced dovecote.

The climb back up the slope was more difficult. Leather soles and drizzle covered grass are not a good combination, and we split into three parties soon after a little birdmanship forecast the first Wren song for 03.43 hours and it came at 03.47 hours. I took the middle group and David Jenkins took up the rear pushing his crumach behind him and using his free hand to push the rear of a lady in front. We met at the top at 04.30 hours, getting back to camp at 05.00 hours, and half an hour later I was asleep. The morning was rather inactive with fog and low cloud. The Wren at Tobar Childa has young fledged, and it seems that once they are controlled vagrants, they are tolerated in other territories. We were invited to 'vagrate' to a wee party at the Trust at 21.30 hours and had enjoyment listening to music from two chanters. Their boat is due tomorrow.

June 12

Messing meeting was boisterous but pleasantly eventful. I decided to leave any variation until tomorrow. The Trust party boat had not come; but, in spite of the weather forecast (the wireless gave us warning of weather we had had yesterday), expected it to come later. I was sitting with David at the Gap when we saw the boat coming in so we had to hurry back to see them off at 17.15 hours.

At 19.30 when the sea was slack, I went with Jim and David across to Dun on the cutter, returning at 22.15 hours after two hours on the island being besieged by Fulmars, and some of which I caught with a noose Finlay fashion. Neither were very happy on the terrain.

June 13

Rations issued this morning so I was late in meeting David on the top. We both went into the glen together, did our own photography and then met up on the Cambir, self having gone via the Well of Virtues and ringed some young Starlings. We decided it was not possible to do the Guillemot counts on the Stacs in Soay Sound as planned and went back to the Lover's stone via the inland cliffs, collecting wool on the way. The LCT left the Long Island during the evening and was expected here during the early hours of the morning.

June 14

Sunday. Soon after I got up David was heard packing in anticipation of an early departure, but high tide was not until midday and there was no chance of beaching until tea time. After sorting my mail, meeting the visitors, arranging meals, washing sheets, preparing bedrooms, doing the Met. at the special request of Benbecula airport and seeing to some minor jobs, I was able to sit down to lunch, which we were taking in two sittings. A number of civilians had landed to stay a few days, two to repair the Decca and two the Marconi. Eric Duffy was swapping with David. Time to shout 'Happy Birthday' to my sister but she can't hear me.

As soon as the stores came off, Rhodes and I handled the rations and put most of the meat into deep freeze as soon as possible. Low tide was at 18.30 hours and after supper those departing climbed into the cutter to get back to the boat, whose bows were now awash above the ramp.

June 15

The LCT left in the early hours. During the morning I entered the Rations up in the books and after lunch took Eric, an ex Swordfish pilot converted to a spider specialist, up to the deep heather clumps on the Conachair side of the enclosures to get some specimens. We circled around to the ledge overlooking Stac a Langa, and the Ard Uachdarchd talus, all near the Gap.

June 16

I got up at 04.15 hours with the intention of doing a singing Wren count in the village, but the wind was too strong to be accurate. Before going back to bed I caught a sheep and removed most of its excess wool so felt well pleased with my half hour out of bed. When normal rising time arrived the wind was still blowing, though it did not reach gale force (f. 8) until late afternoon. Most of the day was spent in the MI room but Eric and I did a 'grass grazing' round in the village after tea.

June 17

It blew hard most of the day in spite of an early frontal passage, but anyhow future weather prospects seemed bright. We went around collecting in the long grass behind the moraine in front of the quarry after tea. My success was moderate but at least I found a species that Eric had not. Prospects for the *Mull* to fetch the Decca mechanics tomorrow are fair.

June 18

A bright day with a long heavy swell from the NW. We were doing a test firing of one of the rockets that we had had alarms with. A big swoosh and I got my binocs onto the sea to see a plume of water rising in the area about 5000 yards short of the pair of Spanish trawlers. We then went home via the hillside, meeting neat sheep lying in the sun, and had earlier seen tup clubs with thickening at the shoulder level and heavier bellies suggesting fat deposition.

June 19

They were due to fire again at 15.30 hours. We both pulled and scrambled our way up the gully opposite the Mess, making full use of the hawser up Mullach Sgar. The lofty serrated tops of the Cuillins of Skye were behind Levenish, and low lying Benbecula showing as a thin line of sand well to the right. Firing was again delayed half an hour because of the number of trawlers who were casually fishing in the target area, but when the button was pressed all went well, the splash being visible by 'naked' eye, with binoculars and the old twin eyed Gunner range finder, and the radar. No resting musicians to hit this time!

Eric and I walked onto Mullach Mor and then went down to the tunnel at the eastern end of the bay. He started back before me to do some collecting on the return journey. He is a good companion and good for me in that as a battle tinged Fleet Air Arm pilot he calmly contributes his experience to the situation as I provide it. At 18.00 hours I was slowly making my way up the Mullach Mor slope of the glen, but still aiming for the crossing point at Am Blaid, with numerous Lesser Black backed Gulls diving at me with extended legs a few feet from my head. Eric came up to join me and we got back in time for supper.

June 20

Ration day again and it was extended into a gentle afternoon. After tea I took Eric and George the conventional way to Carn Mor. Mullach Bi looked particularly beautiful in the late sun. We slid down the gully. Puffins stood in great numbers shifting from foot to foot and nodding, and sometimes, with a little preliminary wing 'undoing' setting off to fly and join the clockwise circling throng above. As we traversed the boulder slopes, a clear area appeared around us, the disturbed birds coming over like Grouse or low flying aeroplanes pressing home their attack oblivious of their ultimate destiny. Eric thought 'a rain' of Puffins an applicable collective noun. There were several thousand present. At 18.15 hours Eric had done some collecting of spiders but we offered him as a bonus a visit to the subterranean Shearwater collection 21ft below us. There were only a few birds sitting but he found some interesting specimens at a depth where the human eyes take a quarter of an hour to acclimatise. We returned along the cliff path and George brought the kitchen back to life with a late supper (with one of us issuing the food and one cooking it how could we fail at such an hour?).

One patient waiting. A Guillemot with worms, which was dosed with Piperazine and soon took fish out of the hand.

June 21 (Sunday) and June 22 (Monday)

Choose which day you want for the Equinox. I have never been constant in my choice, but once again we turn around. Tennis at Cowglen Military Hospital continued until 23.15 hours and had there been Shearwaters and Petrels in Glasgow we would have set off for the City's equivalent of Carn Mor after the last game. The BBC Island Naturalist Programme at Sunday lunch broadcast the recordings taken on Carn Mor and on Boreray. The clatter of beer cans on Carn Mor was not a feature. With the news that the sick Guillemot will now take fish off the floor, and delicately pick up tiny remnants off a surface, such important information concentrates the mind on the expectations of the 23rd when the UK's first Corporal was to be fired: towards us. We await the promised accuracy.

CHAPTER NINE

....

'Stormy' Petrel and Burrow

'X' Hour

June 23

'X' hour was at 16.00 hours, but, owing to a small delay it was not until 16.25 hours that the Corporal missile left its launching platform: to us only a noise, but to the spectators on South Uist a sight not easy to forget: or so we hoped. Eric and I, with binoculars as a Unit fall back, had decided to take our perch in front of the DRF (Direction Range Finding) building, a position from where we would know which way to look and also hear the count down over the loud speakers in the building.

Leaving the camp at 14.00 hours we walked along to Dun passage where *Laminaria* seaweed hung limp in the calm low water. A common seal sat on a rock and watched inquisitively as we picked our way across the rocks in a half hearted attempt to reach Dun. My route failed me though I would have done it with perseverance, but Eric at least was able to say he had been on Dun, even though the part he had sat on showed no promise for further ascent.

A Shackleton flew low over the target area under the thin but irritating cloud which covered it patchily, and hid our tops more securely. When walking up the slopes towards Decca the cloud became thicker and momentarily even Levenish was dimmed in our view.

'The time is X minus 15 ... now' and this was followed by the final countdown with the words leading to 'missile away' being almost obscured by the swoosh of the missile leaving its pad. For twenty or more seconds nothing was seen or heard. The Radar aerials swung in rhythm, and white clouds puffed around and below us, leaving a large expanse of blue above for eyes to watch. High up a vapour trail appeared; it broke, twisted, and then restarted, finally shutting off altogether as the missile, now free of its fuel, continued on its way. Three minutes later the countdown to expected burst begun and after twenty seconds it must have fallen, for a loud bang with a secondary shock wave was heard.

None of us saw it! Eric had been present at the target end at Ascension Island when the first American Intercontinental Missile had its trial, and was present here also for our smaller one! Both of us spent a few less important minutes watching a newly fledged family of Wrens flying around on the boulder beach. This was while watching the Guillemot off the slipway when it had been discharged from the MI room as 'fit to return to duty'. It had made much splashing and attracted swooping Gulls, but each time done a timely dive of evasion.

A Fishery Research vessel came into the bay during the evening and we got some fish off it, George Maclellan, Sgt. Tombes and myself were up to 00.30 hours gutting them. The same Sgt. who had manned the DRF at 'X' hour, and was the only Guinness drinker to overwinter. A moderate drinker, he never quite finished the supply sent on the last boat: a dozen gross instead of a gross.

June 24

Having been in bed 2 hours, I rose at 03.00 hours and walked up to the Gap to see the sunrise from Conachair. The first Wren song was at 03.20 hours from the enclosures and five minutes later they started at Ard Uarachdar. To the left of Boreray Stacs was a crimson glow from a hidden sun; a glow that had probably been present all night, local midnight being at 01.30 BST.

I sat on a grass ledge 30 or 40ft down near the Gap with growling Guillemots to my right, and Fulmars gliding as if with 'frozen' wings in front. On a grass ledge further down near the Gap, without egg or scrape, sat a particularly aggressive bird, shooting oil furiously at any would be site pincher. A Puffin crept out of its hole and surveyed the world. Presumably it had other reasons for sitting there than merely sitting waiting for the sun to rise. The air was still and warm and at 04.35 hours. I got up and walked along the cliff, the densely coloured sunlit clouds now lying over Boreray. Elsewhere the sky was a pale powder blue with a few high fleecy clouds above me, tinged creamy yellow, and cumuliform behind me coloured pink. At 05.10 hours a bright orange spot appeared on the horizon, heralded perhaps by some low horizon cloud appearing to reflect a fire below.

It rose slowly, not as the midwinter sun over the Manse but as if it was tired through lack of sleep. For a minute it was bisected by cloud, and then for a briefer moment hung almost uncovered. My camera shutter released, the sun slowly hid behind thicker cloud, and I turned back down to camp well satisfied.

We breakfasted at 07.30 hours for the next 'X' was at noon. The LCT arrived in the bay. I had seen it coming from my perch at 04.00 hours, its mast light barely moving from the vertical, so calm was the sea. It now lay in the bay, the mail was removed, and a decision needed to be made as to when we were going to unload the 150 x 40 gallon drums of diesel. It would have suited us to wait, but not the LCT. They had their weekend of frolicking at Helensburgh to get back to! She insisted on beaching, and from 11.30 hours those lads not on 'X' were working, pushing and rolling diesel drums. Some bright spark had tipped them all out of their trailers!

At 13.40 hrs I started walking up the road in order to be at the DRF by 14.00 hours, and having got to Am Blaid in 15 minutes, my record time, and to the building 3 minutes later it was to discover that a hold up of 15 minutes had been ordered. I lay in the sun with the sea mist alternatively thinning and thickening. Visibility was just over 8,000 yards, but above was a cloudless sky, and as 'missile away' rang out we watched expectantly for the trails high above us. Once again they showed clearly and then it was all eyes on the sea. It landed 10 secs. after the expected burst and I missed it by 2 secs., or rather missed the first 2 secs. of the splash which was seen by Sgt. Tombes on the DRF. At 10 miles range the splash from the water falling from the first splash looked large, but the initial one must have been about 400ft high. The secondary splash was about 100 to 150 yards wide and easily visible with the naked eye once the binocs had identified the point of fall. Having given the Met. conditions I went down to Skipper Ian on the LCT to explain why things were going so slowly, fetched drinks for the lads, and supervised their work from the safety aspect, as dropping and rolling drums off the trailers which we had had to load them onto off the Crafts ramp, could have presented problems. The LCT ramp was lifted so as to be 3ft off the sand so that they rolled straight on to the trailers, and these could be pulled up our 'moth eaten' shore ramp by wire hawsers. It was very hot, and work continued while the LCT crew bathed and watched us.

Low tide was at 16.00 hours, and from 19.30 hours onwards the Skipper had had to push the craft up the beach to keep her grounded. Eric had decided to return on this one rather than be late should one not come for a week, and I was sorry to see him go, having learnt much ecological thought and method from him. We were all very tired in the evening and glad of our beds.

June 25

Low cloud, drizzle and sticky hot air did not make a pleasant day until later on we had rain. We moved rations into the store and entered them up. At 14.45 hours the Barra Lifeboat, £37,500 of it, came into the bay at the end of a training cruise, bringing several passengers with them for the trip. Barra is very much Roman Catholic (*the dividing line between the Protestant north and RC south lies across Benbecula. The arrival of two Fathers was geographical and they were not looking for me, however the Postal bosses were*).

The Director of Scottish Postal Services and also The Chief Postmaster of South Uist were keen to see what they were in charge of, and how the medics lightened their load. I took this party around the village, brought them back for tea, seeing them off at 16.30 hours with a crew that had supplemented their Vitamin B intake by forcing down beer and Guinness ('Have Faith Fathers, have faith').

June 26

The Messing meeting had again failed to materialise; so I stopped them.

There was no hard feeling on either side. The only grumbles I ever heard were about the excessive amount of crab dishes on the menus. The menus for the week are discussed when the Rations are issued on a Saturday and the chefs are so motivated and bright that repetition is rare.

Rain and low cloud most of the day.

June 27

LCT expected tomorrow. During the latter part of the afternoon I started to make up the 200ft mist net to catch some birds in the village. I have started mounting my transparencies in glass.

June 28

Sunday. A day in which low cloud and rain removed all memories of summer. Capt. Bob Bradman came off the LCT and after lunch I walked up to the Marconi doing it in the record time of 25 mins up the road.

We were unable to get the Radar 4 Mark 7 down in these conditions so the LCT will not leave until tomorrow. John Leach and Peter Jones, Skipper and No. 1 came off for drinks in the evening.

June 29

I took Bob around the village once my MI room work was completed. After lunch we go a lift up to where the Mark 7 was being prepared for its journey down the hill, and then walked up to Mullach Sgar, veering right to get on to the Col and then up Conachair. Bob treated the top edge with great respect, using his posterior as a means of progression. Our tea was late and the main supper early, as the LCT beached at 18.00 hours. She never quite dried out but on slack tide at 19.18 hours the new Radar was dragged out into a mere nine inches of water by Scammel, with the tractor giving an extra pull up the beach to the top. The old one was put on half an hour later and by 21.30 hours Bob and the other returning passengers were on board.

June 30

The meat taken off the LCT was put in the deep freeze last night, and the fresh veg was dealt with this morning. After tea I went with Maclellan up to the Gap as the sun was inviting. The grass was wet and we could not get to our usual perch because we were in gym shoes. We had to get a differential count of Guillemots done and by sliding down we got to a fresh discovered grass ledge beyond our previous limit, from where we could see Stac a Langa. There was no possibility of returning the same way, so we turned left to the NE towards a point above Mol Ghiasgar and rejoined the usual route upwards, then going back down to the Gap and village. Before supper I cut my hair, getting no adverse comment in the Mess.

July 1

I was digging soon after 08.00 hours in order to produce a hole big enough to hold the contents of the first chamber of the cesspit and the grease trap. 20 minutes digging gave me an uncomfortable hunger and I was ready for breakfast. Rain failed to hold up the operation when it was dug and we finished by 11.00 hours.

The rest of the morning and up to teatime was spent tidying up the MI room and after tea I did a village walk and there was enough light for me to continue to use David Jenkins's Kodachrome film.

The grass in the village is now long, the sheep are fat especially the tups, and most of them oozing lethargy which is only interrupted by occasional butting matches. Here a tup raises his lip, extends his head and advances towards a ewe. Too early! But worth practicing.

July 2

After a promising evening last night, frontal conditions this morning were a little disappointing. Up to now it was understood that the LCT was coming on Sunday, bringing Brigadier Hennersey, the Director of Medical Services for Scotland, who was based in Edinburgh, a Brigadier Royal Engineers, our own Col. Cooper and a few minor 'swanners'. The NAAFI manager had been put off (*was it on grounds of status?*). On Tuesday *H.M.S. Adamant*, the submarine depot ship, is due with James Fisher the ornithologist and author (*the NN book on the Fulmar Petrel*), Col. Retd. Ian Grant the younger of Rothiemurchus, Mr Arbuthnot from the NTS, Jeffrey Boswell BBC (again) and a number of officers and men wanting to see St Kilda. James is talented and skilled, has Oundle connections, failed to answer a letter I wrote to him and is said to be unreliable. Ian Grant I have met while helping out Edinburgh OTC on a winter warfare course in the Cairngorms, and I knew little of my own DDMS.

News came through this morning that both boats are arriving on Tuesday, and that the LTC is bringing 6000 gallons of POL, and this day is also an 'X' missile day! We certainly have activity and variety in it. Fortunately God should be with us as two Service Chaplains of Colonel status have decided to come on the *Adamant*.

We had a Norman Wisdom film in the evening. Perhaps he should be invited to join us on Tuesday.

July 3

The medical team of a Private NO, a Sgt. NO and myself went through the MI room and did yet another drug check to please the Brigadier. Sgt. Murphy knew him slightly and remembered how he liked his whisky but Capt. Will Warner the OC only knew his own Colonel. There seemed a possibility that he and I would not be recognising each other's visitors. Low cloud and drizzle confined me to our part of the island with plenty to do.

July 4

I spent the morning issuing Rations. After lunch I went out with George Mac, and we collected as many flowers as we could find on a transect from the Factor's House through the village to Tobar Childa and on to the moraine under Glacan Conachair. Here we found a lamb tangled in loose signals line which, when half freed raced down below us, leading a bunch of sheep into wild panic. My attempts to catch it were of no avail, and half an hour later we lost it above Tobar Childa. After tea two floras with a 'cheat book' came out and without a break for supper we worked right through until well after 22.00 hours, identifying twenty one species in this time.

July 5

Sunday. I reviewed some of our identifications this morning. Clouds still hung over the hills but there was hope of a cold front passing today, and I was not going to be kept back any more. Am Blaid was free of cloud but more was forming on the wind as it rushed up the west cliffs. I took the inland route to the Cambir, but instead of walking along under the West Cliffs, walked with some difficulty along the top of them, for the grass was wet and I wanted to look into the Fulmar's nests.

I walked along the east side of the Cambir but spent half an hour at the near bottom of a grassy slope by Sgeir na Caraidh counting Guillemots and Kittiwakes. Having reached the end at around 17.25 hours the sky suddenly cleared, low cloud leaving the hills; and an expanse of blue cloud coming up from the SW gave us hopes.

July 6

There is still some doubt about the details of tomorrow's loads but the MI room is highly presentable.

July 7

Just before *H.M.S. Adamant*, the 16,000 ton submarine depot ship steamed around Oiseval, we heard that the *Mull* had left Loch Carnan and Brig. RE and Brig. RAMC were definitely on board.

From just above the pier the stern of *Adamant* only occasionally showed clear of Oiseval as she swung on her bow anchor in the tide. For the first time for many days there was no rain. After ten minutes a hole appeared in her side, and into a boat lowered from above climbed about a dozen people, mostly in civilian dress. This drew away, cutting through the gentle swell and rounding our yellow buoy, slowly came along the rope. Jeffrey Boswell was the only one there I recognised but the main cause for concern was the sight of an unexpected

Brigadier, who introduced himself as though his arrival had been known for many months beforehand. Brigadier Cameron was Chief of Staff Scottish Command, a tall man with a ruddy complexion. Everyone was shown up to mess where tea all round was distributed, and gratefully accepted. James Fisher had not come but there were more NTS staff than expected. James Arbuthnot is the Nature Conservancy land agent.

The Earl of Wemyss headed the NTS party which included Admiral Angus Cunningham Graham, Lord Doune, the eldest son of the Earl of Galloway, and Michael Crichton Stewart from Falkland Palace, Fife.

At about 11.00 hours I started taking these, with several others including the Captain from the *Adamant*, around the village. All were very pleasant, but expected different answers from me, according to their role. They seemed surprised with what I could tell them, but I had got the advantage of ten months behind me.

Sgt. Murphy RAMC was taking the chaplains down the village street, and like me was in rolled up shirt sleeve order. By noon a few boatloads of sailors had landed. Ian Grant had briefed himself well. It was Christmas 1957 that he had hosted the EUOTC at his house where we first met, self acting as MO to the winter warfare course.

We returned for lunch soon after 13.00 hours but all the non-army visitors eat a packed lunch on the cliff edge outside the Mess. Fortunately the LTC with more loose diesel drums had postponed its visit until Thursday, but we still had the missile to cope with for 'X' hour was 16.30 hours.

After lunch the liberty boat several times disgorged a number of sailors who, appreciative of some space, rushed off in different directions shouting, chasing each other or bowling stones *ad lib* down the slopes into the sea. At 15.00 hours my group got a lift up top and then went on to Conachair. I decided to walk up to my DRF post via the Bailey bridge, Ruaival and Decca. Seeing the Church of Scotland minister on the way I invited him to come with me, and although well above middle age, with a zigzag path we managed the climb (*my notes quote MY Pastoral staff. I cannot recall ever using one so it should read HIS*) getting a lift (both on duty) from Decca to the DRF. 'X' was put off half an hour, but although there was too much cloud to see the trail in the sky, the splash at 15,000 yards was clearly visible being c. 400ft high.

Once back at camp we accepted an invitation to get some of our soldiers on to the *Adamant* in the evening for some entertainment, so this meant a change of clothes and only a suit was at hand. I arrived at the Recreation room just after the start of a Joint Church Service. This ended at 18.30 hours and I had taken communion with the Brig., the OC Will, and a Bombardier after the main service.

Ten minutes later we were in the boat on the way out to ship, leaving Jeffrey behind to explore the island further (he had made a brief landing on Stac an Armin during the afternoon). Once on board we were ushered into the Ward Room and I was not surprised to find all civilians in dinner jackets and the naval personnel in No. Ones. While we were drinking the *Mull* was coming up past Levenish and a quarter of an hour later I left to greet the arriving Brigadiers on the pier. With a certain amount of ceremony, far exceeding that in the *Mull* or LCTs I was ushered off down the companion way to the cutter and across to the *Mull* to collect the two Brigs., Hennersey and Lord Napier of Magdala and take them to the Mess where some whisky was arranged by Sgt. Murphy 'to settle their stomachs, sir'. We then all had supper while those on the *Adamant* dined there. They returned an hour later when I handed over the role of host to Will but not in time to warn him that the Chief Engineer was also a peer, and he should sustain the polite conversation he had used in the Ward Room. We were relieved to get them to bed.

July 8

It was raining hard when I got up and continued to do so until the cold front passed over during the morning. Until break time we cleared up the MI room and at 10.45 hours I started taking the Brigadier RAMC around, first touring the kitchens where George Mac was on duty and then the Medical Centre where the experienced Sgt. Murphy was behind my right shoulder with his soft Glaswegian Irish accent to add comments to work that ranged from dentistry to removing tattoos. I made a special point of the section of my own room being used as a laboratory to examine and ring birds. He had probably heard about this and gave a gentle approving smile; a smile of satisfaction and amusement. It was gently raining so waterproofs were donned for the inspection of the cesspit and grease trap. After this I left him to his own devices in the Mess and arranged to finish some of my mail, as the *Mull* intended to sail at 14.00 hours with the last of our visitors. Pork for lunch, and soon after we escorted the VIPs to the pier to get them into the dory in a fairly calm sea. The remainder of the afternoon was occupied in recovering. It had not been stressful but we had found it different in that so much of our stress is either through a natural event such as landing a boat in a heavy sea or by self organised stress. Recovery itself is a tedious process and for my part the tedium was eased by taking the three NC students up to the Gap and back via Tobar Childa.

July 9

While clearing the trap lines set by the students last night I was able to discuss the various insular differences of mice and Starlings in the north. I then invigilated Sgt. Tutts' GCE Ordinary Maths Exam in the Medical Centre. This finished at 13.00 hours, soon after which LCT 4071 came onto the beach at about 8 knots, grounding impressively.

During the afternoon the diesel was unloaded and I continued to complete all the forms associated with the exam paper. After tea I walked down with Percy to put him on the LCT and he left with a greasy handshake; greasy because I had just been putting the meat in the deep freezer.

July 10

Today was an 'X' day, the hour being 12.30 hours. I walked up leisurely with the students, taking them over the maritime grassland (*Plantago coronopus* complex) and on to the *Nardus* area higher up from Decca towards Ruaival.

At the DRF we did not have to wait long for the 'X' minus 15 count, and visibility was fairly good, however at 'X' minus 4 there was a hold and after announcing that it would not recommence until 14.00 hours we set off down the hill to return for a quick lunch. At 13.35, after a heavy lunch, I struggled up the gully, reaching the top in 18 minutes and walked over to the DRF. There were more holds and the wind was getting stronger with the warm front on us by 15.00 hours. By 16.00 hours visibility was down to 7,000 yards and it was due to land at 10,000 yards from us, but soon after take off it apparently burst into flames and made a premature entry into the sea in front of the Secretary of State, Christopher Soames and numerous other VIPs. This was the first 'press invite day' and it would be that the first upset was in their view. Our RT informally picked up that the press had been told that it had been blown up to show that it could be if need be.

July 11

Having no 'telescopic' lens for my camera I had to seek close ups of birds and sheep by stalking them. It seems there was time, light, and clouds today, and having done the rations early I spent much time photographing.

July 12

Sunday. I spent the morning indoors, there being rain and low cloud, blowing gale before lunch, declining in the afternoon and restarting in the evening producing the odd rampant empty diesel drum and dustbin.

At 13.40 George Mac and myself decided on a quick tour of Conachair. Going via Tobar Childa we climbed through the mist up the ravines and gullies of Glacan Conachair, getting to the top by about 14.40 hours. The wind was strong and made it hard for us to get to Marconi across the Col. From there we went to the DRF, and returned to camp via the cliff edge, the boulder beach and then to the road. The film 'From Here to Eternity' with Deborah Kerr in the evening. Great.

July 13

Little bursts of sunshine during the day enabled me to take more photos, but I lost my UV filter on the boulder storm beach. I walked clockwise around the village back to the Factor's House. During the evening I walked around Oiseval to photograph the radiant aura over the Outer Hebrides, and later up to Am Blaid to photograph the sun setting at 22.30 hours.

July 14

I included in my photographs today House No. 2, where Finlay MacQueen once lived. The name Norman MacQueen is inscribed in the cement plaster. At 22.45 hours George and myself took the three Nature Conservancy Students off to Carn Mor (*no trip to this fine talus slope is too familiar to the leader. To those that know it the way is safe in good conditions, 'interesting' to the first timer, and workable with nets so that, at the right place, Storm Petrels, Leach's (Fork tailed) Petrel and Manx Shearwater can be introduced to visitors by hand. Each trip has different highlights, but for guidance details see the other visits*).

Tonight we found a grey fluffy chick in the underground cavern, ringed three Leach's, and five Manxies, and found our way back two strange ways, self having to use a loose fallen telephone line to decide which was north and which south. Bed at 04.00 hours pleased that I had found my filter earlier in the day. I also cut my hair today and was complimented.

July 16

Yesterday's firing had been put off until 13.45 hours today but the weather is bad now with heavy rain, a thunderstorm and low cloud.

After tea it stopped raining and I took the students out to do some mist netting in a wet area hoping to catch some Snipe. Even a long wader net failed to catch any. Will had seen a Heron in a weak condition but it flew strongly away from me.

July 17

Weather looks a little promising today. When I got up at 07.00 hours the LCT was on the beach but the doors were still up, and it was not for two hours that they started unloading. She was then quite dry and I went on board to ask the Skipper for cocoa at 09.45 hours. Pelham Clinton a (titled) micro lepidopterist came off as did another student as replacement for the one leaving.

Having sorted my mail we all had cocoa in the Mess. I took a rare lift up to the DRF but found there was a further hold up and decided to go down to the bottom again. The burst was intended for 4,500 yards, the nearest to us yet. After supper I went up again to find some of the lads had been there since 08.00 hours. The call 'missile away' came at 23.15 hours, while I was standing outside Decca looking towards South Uist. A few seconds elapsed and a bright yellow glow, as intense and bigger than a lighthouse lantern slowly rose above the horizon veering slightly to the left, entering the first cloud layer to reappear before finally vanishing into thick cloud above, giving this a slight glow. From this nothing was seen or heard until we had been told that it had been blown up by Range Safety. Later we heard that this was specifically done in our interest. Thank you Range Safety.

July 18

Ration issue this morning, good hot curry for lunch, and was ready to receive the *Mull* as she steamed into the bay. Major Macgregor came along for the trip and Pt. Higgins came to relieve Pt. Rhodes. Most of the so called operational staff were on the trip to await the rocket. They had to wait until later in the evening when a loud bang as it dropped 22,000 yards away worried some of the visiting staff.

Mac left during the evening at 23.00 hours and I rowed him out to the *Mull* with the Skipper and our plumber. An almost full moon illuminated the village and reflected off the water as bright yellow patches under the island of Dun at the southern side of the bay. Even the *Mull* under such conditions looked pretty, but having been up and not exactly static since 07.00 hours, my destination was bed.

July 19

Sunday. It rained most of the day and the wind got up at lunch time, reaching gale force about mid afternoon. I spent much time in the unit dark room printing some of my negatives. After a film in the evening, 'The Cockleshell Heroes', the wind veered from SE to SW, which gave hope of better weather.

July 20

Work inside most of the morning but took a pre-lunch stroll. At 15.00 hours George and I walked up to the crossroads, taking short cuts across the bends, and came out just east of Claigan Mor, eventually taking a long steep grassy slope leading down to Rudha M'hurich. Here we were 300ft above the sea. The intention was to climb around the West Cliffs as low as possible and get to Carn Mor, and this we adhered to, covering ground where we had not been before. The vegetation was very lush, much of it having an ungrazed appearance. By a devious route we came down onto Laimrig nan Gall, 361ft (the foreigner's landing place), having come down from a promontory 600ft above. The topographical interest here is that from above it seems access is only really possible through a 20ft gap from the sea: hence possibly the name. As far as is known this is a very rarely visited area and no account can be found of it. We continued along the lower slopes, arriving on the boulder slope of Carn Mor about 17.00 hours. There were some dead Puffin and Shearwater chicks among the boulders. We returned up the cliff path getting back for a late supper.

July 21

Another 'X' hour today but it was not fired until later in the evening. After lunch I went with George M up past the enclosures and on to the Gap, from where we hoped to get on to a lower ledge by getting back up Oiseval and going down one of the gullies onto a lower path, but the sorrel was too wet and although we almost got there, further progress would have been dangerous. We have been thwarted twice: but at least thwarted by common sense, and we safely made our way to the top of Oiseval and came down windy ridge and 'hit' the path to the left of the organ loft, this way taking us towards the Gap and Rudh Gill – The Point.

Around Oiseval the sheep have two legs longer on one side than the other. Anyone questioning this had better try and go around it.

July 22

The landing craft that had twice brought me to the island arrived just after lunch, but this time it was skippered by Major Charles, who has the reputation of hitting the beach delightfully hard with everything except his underpants flying from the mast.

Frank Green the Meteorological Officer from the Nature Conservancy had come to see my Met. set up, and Major Dixon, Army Catering Corps of Scot. Co. came to see how we did the Rations. He had priority so I spent most of the afternoon explaining the history, development and organisation of the ration system here.

Frank came ashore for the night and we got several points discussed during the evening, for while I had been occupied during the afternoon he had been looking through my records. Others spent the afternoon unloading diesel drums from the

LCT. After the evening film we had the students in for drinks as it was Crocket's 21ˢᵗ.

July 23

Just before 10.00 hours Driver Davies drove Frank and myself up top in a 1 toner into thick cloud on top of Mullach Mor. We could see very little from the top and walked down to the village getting to the Mess soon after 11.00 hours. After lunch I had more chances to talk to Frank, Major Dixon and Pelham Clinton before they went on board at 18.30 hours with the boat dry up to midships with the low spring tides. We went on board for drinks in the Ward Room and got back for supper late.

I later learned that both my main contacts had been well pleased with the work done by the RAMC team in their non medical roles. Frank later got an academic post at Oxford. The gap between Pelham Clinton and myself was due to my lack of knowledge of micro and macro Moths; a gap that is still huge.

July 24

A day off for all today. George and I made it a long afternoon to explore unknown parts around Ard Uachdarachd. The first part of the walk as far as the Gap and across the scree slope onto the east side of this promontory, was not new, but once at the point, with the cleit above us, the green slopes led steeply down below us, we were in new ground. Here were sheep who never knew flat ground, and during the winter saw little sun. Now they saw us with slight alarm. To our left above us stood Conachair; 400 yards away and frighteningly great. Lower we went, our posteriors doing most of the sliding, and feet and fingers dug deep into the thick turf. Once the steep slope changed to cliff face we turned right and took a small path which allowed us to overlook some more grass below. The only way down was along a narrow muddy track, probably not trodden by humans for over 30 years. It lost little height but took us to a point where a left hairpin turns across some sorrel slopes, a short contour with a gully on our right, and a shorter climb up to a crest left us in full possession of the small grass slope below us. A few minutes later we retraced our way to the hairpin and instead of turning right back went straight on. Our destination was a small promontory, two thirds of the height of Ard Uachdarachd. Sheep ahead of us turned and sped back past us. There could be no way around! This was getting less pleasurable and we chose to retreat to less challenging work and climbed back via the top of Conachair, from where we could see the peaks of Harris, Benbecula, the summits of Skye, North Uist, and South Uist each with their tops producing fine orographic cloud, and standing out as clear as for many weeks. How many times in the future will I stand on these and look on beloved Hirta, 'All alone and yet alive'. Our backs turned on the summit and we went on to the col. It was warm and after a photo of what we had left we went back down the road.

July 25

I continue to send thrice daily AERO reports to Benbecula and every so often they send for a special. Presumably the firing range are getting their reports of the weather here from Benbecula as they never contact us direct. Benbecula then get it from us. Rations this morning and netted a Snipe in body moult this afternoon.

July 26

Low cloud cleared up in late morning and George Mac and myself walked up to Am Blaid in a complete calm and warm and sticky atmosphere, both dripping in sweat. We crossed the North Glen half way up its height. A few almost feathered Gull chicks scuttled ahead of us and squatted, with parents calling accusingly from overhead.

We climbed out of the glen, onto the cliff/slope which I had been down solo recently and which shall now be called Geo Furasda or the Accessible Inlet, for it is in reality a long grass slope leading down to an inlet with Kittiwakes and Guillemots on the far side, and Fulmars on its less steep boulder strewn ledges, where damp sorrel and puking chicks make travelling uncomfortable. We devised a method of grabbing neck and beak to prevent ourselves getting oiled and holding one leg out to have a ring applied.

July 27

A day of drizzle and low cloud, a short village walk and catching up writing records.

July 28

I am making a big effort to catch as many mice as possible to get more recaptured. The 'chippy' thought he had seen a party of rats, the first one coming off the LCT on July 9, but Murphy and myself set traps and lit fires with no signs. LCT expected tomorrow with a Signals Locating Team.

July 29

The boat came just before supper and unloaded even more people than expected, for two US Army Sergeants arrived with a US Army Officer, called Cochran. Major Alan Needham, the REME boss from Benbecula also came for the day.

After supper there was the usual rush of opening mail, answering it and putting it out for post. The new officers were entered. The three students left us and went back on board fairly early, but Alan went back on the dory around 23.00 hours after a noggin session in the Mess. Some of my heavy luggage went off in today's boat, as also did the 13lbs of wool that I had collected, mainly off Frederick the late dominant pale tup of the village, but also some dark ewes. This was sent to Mrs Maclellan for her to arrange spinning.

July 30

The traps were not set last night so I thought I would get ahead in schedule by starting on the rations. I did really well and finished entering and lifting them by lunchtime. The ration issue for next week has also been calculated.

When will the sun appear? This afternoon I wandered around An Lag Bho'n Tuath (The northern valley or 'enclosures' (*the northern glen is Gleann Mor leading down to Glen Bay*)). At the enclosures the heather (collective term for Ling and other *Calluna species*) was in full flower where it has always grown thicker on the Conachair side of the enclosures which is better drained and provides a dry soft bed where I lay and closed my eyes silently taking in the sounds around me. A Raven calling overhead soon gave me up as potential carrion and a pair of Oystercatchers, one with a broken voice, no longer piped or swooped at me. A long line of ewes which had come up from Tobar Childa crept along a few yards beneath me, none with any eyes or ears for the motionless prone figure.

'Fling me into September, for all is too lush for so little sun'. If Hirta can carpet her hills with grass and heather as green as this when mist and cloud smother her from above, then her powers exceed all ours, and no one will understand her. For nearly a year I have felt her soil, tramped her hills and scrambled around her cliffs, and she still surrenders not her inmost secrets. So many short affairs have breathed inaccuracies; and if there are those who deny this, then she has won.

July 31

On April 25 my walk along the slopes of the west cliffs had been brought to an abrupt end by a gully which would have needed some negotiating. The path we had been following led to an old very rotten plank across the top of this gully where the gully ended against a 20ft 80 degree smooth rock face. George and I had decided that the gully fell away to the sea for about 400ft as a grassy slope, and that the slope up above the face of rock was first tussocky then with craggy rock. This site is to the north of Carn Mor and where we were, this plank was the old crossing of a gully top with about 400ft of alternative terrains above and 400ft below. Neither slope was sheer, but did not look comfortable; but neither would I have fancied the 8 to 9ft plank as a fowler! The sides of the gully both continued upwards, enclosing the tussocky area as ridges and there were two great clefts in these, both of which we used to get through the rock ridges. The path between clefts had fallen away in two places, but if it held a sheep it would hold us on all fours. It did.

Ten profitable minutes were spent exploring a higher path (two cleits also found during this crossing) and soon the link with the Cambir was visible. We had been slowly moving north the whole time and at last the going was easy. We returned along the cliff tops above Geo na Stacan (the bay of the stacs), well pleased with our traverse of the steep slopes we could see below us, which had taken three hours. Supper was very welcome even though I had had a large mackerel for lunch.

August 1

Ration issue during the morning. At 14.30 hours in a very calm sea we set of for Dun, rowing because the Seagull engine had again broken down. Half an hour later George Maclellan, Major Farmen, Royal Signals, and the US Army Lieutenant Cochran and myself landed easily. The soft spongy terrain was yielding to every step and our two visitors yielded to it and decided to hang around locally. George and I set off for the end of Dun. During the next fifty minutes we slowly made our way across the Fescue/Sorrel covered slopes ringing Fulmars as we went. This is almost an arduous an activity as cleit creeping. Not so dangerous but more uncomfortable: smelly (which is acceptable) and oily, which is less so. If this gets you, your clothes are tainted *ad perpetuam.* We took a good path and arrived beneath the wall, built by hands in a close pattern it denies access to the end, rather supporting the name Dun which means a Fort. Here Shags scuttled like rats in the tunnels beneath the boulders and young Puffins squeaked as their parents made their moans, resembling the rumblings of a hungry 'tummy'. We photographed Puffin and chick, and a Shag with a cross bill deformity. The end of Dun was thoroughly explored and we found a heavy growth of *Atriplex* and *Matricaria* on a small plateau on the south side of the furthest peak. We left an hour for the walk back and met the Major and the Yank just above where the boat was due to come in at 17.45 hours.

August 2

Sunday. There was the chance of a boat today, but it did not materialise. Mid afternoon I took a trip around Oiseval as far as I had explored.

August 3

No boat yesterday but early in the morning we were told that 14.00 hours was a likely ETA, but not to beach, only to bring some Radar spare parts. A visiting officer's crew took the dory out with the OC in the stern and self in the bow. The rowing was erratic and when we arrived we found we were only needed as carriers of the Royal Mail, as they were preparing to use their dory.

After tea I walked up to Decca where I did some work on sea bird flying speeds, having earlier developed ideas on long distance recognition of Gannets and others, based on known routes of species, known times of usage and wave form.

August 4

Today was an 'X' day, but the cloud was very low and there was very little hope of a firing. I got a lift up to the clouds and attended to Cameron's knee in the VHF building, returning along the glen side of Mullach Sgar with a strong wind blowing me against the slope and wet heavy clouds obscuring all but my most immediate surroundings. From Am Blaid the village was not visible, and it was not until I got below Decca that I was able to see the sea in the bay. I returned along the cliffs and boulder beach and got back in time for tea. The weather did not improve during the day.

August 5

In the morning I studied some more of the new forms sent me by Frank Green and later started completing them, having read some of the details last night. Form 3208 is certainly more of a combined presentation than the separate climatological (record of past weather) and synoptic (records to anticipate future weather) and would have suited me from the start, but at the hand over the Army, being non fliers, could not see any need for any thing on the sea, such as a boat, or in the air, such as an anemometer. They refused to take them on their books. Whether my successor who arrives on the *Mull* tonight knows what he will be expected to do, or whether he wants to learn I know not (*I was later complimented on my self set up by the Met. Office*). During the afternoon I walked the village and finished up on the boulder beach watching Major Fairman and a Captain playing cricket – St Kilda version – with MCC syn. Military Cricket Corps rules. After supper we played Liar Dice until the *Mull* came around the corner of Oiseval at 00.00 hours, having already sent a message to say she was encountering heavy swell and could not find the way. What she thought her Radar was for, nobody quite knows. Perhaps to scare the Gulls away.

August 6

We took off Lieut. Hudson the new MO and two NC people, Dr Clarke and Mr Harding soon after midnight. During cocoa I sat with them in the Mess, conversing on their proposed work and then went to bed.

First thing in the morning I showed Richard Hudson around the MI room and we started checking its contents, a laborious process. I also introduced him to the Meteorological recordings.

After tea I took Clark and Harding round the village and Tobar Childa, getting back in time for supper. For a time the clouds cleared and the sun shone across the village. The day again passed without UK 17 leaving her launching pad and tomorrow another attempt will be made, but in spite of this

193

lack of activity the morning was occupied doing mail, and showing the visiting Lieut. Col. A. Q. Scot. Co. around and seeing them all off at 17.00 hours.

August 7

First jobs were sorting my trap lines, checking instruments in MI room, and walking Richard up to the quarry and back past Tobar Childa. Those concerned with the firing were again hopping around as hold after hold was called with varying reasons. It was not until 21.15 hours that the count down started, but this was the final one and was a success. During this time I took my place up top but failed to pick out the flare of the missile leaving.

August 8

Tim Street's LCT arrived in the early hours of the morning and was anchored at the buoy when I came down to breakfast. The few passengers came off during the early morning with the mail and the craft beached at 11.00 hours. I started issuing the rations at 10.00 hours after doing the Met. and a few other jobs, and at lunch time we had only done three quarters of the Ration work. This was partly because I was explaining the procedures to Lieut. Hudson while doing it prior to him taking over the messing when my departure is near. All was finished during the afternoon and I took a short walk. A film during the evening with Michael Redgrave was good. Tim Street and Lieut. Hoad came for drinks afterwards, but I left them at 22.30 hours to change for my nocturnal visit to Carn Mor. I said my goodbyes to visitors and left the camp with George at 22.45 hours, just as dusk had taken over from the light of day. Once at Am Blaid it was dark and the sun just showed as a red glow to the right of Soay. Even now its course below the horizon grows longer and at local midnight, 01.30 hours BST, it was quite dark. Small wisps of cloud hung over Soay. No wind moved them. The face of Mullach Bi was dim in cloud, which, suspended by invisible supports, hardly stirred, so that the peak itself was quite free. We took the usual route but the slope was very wet and slippery. The poles and net were removed from the cleit and we went along to the same grassy avenue that I took the NT to. However the net was rather torn and having set it up we spent the hour from 23.45 hours to 24.45 hours getting dozens of Petrels hitting the net but catching about a third of them. George had the distinction of holding a Leach's in his right hand while his first 'Stormy' fluttered off the ground into his left. By midnight there was as many Shearwaters swooping and crossing over Carn Mor as I had ever seen and occasionally a thump and a quick flutter signified that a bird had located its area, dropped into it, and scuttled to the correct hole.

August 9

Sunday. Still on Carn Mor as expected. We packed the net up, returned the poles to the cleit and slowly walked up to the main Shearwater colony, looking for birds sitting on the rocks, black shapes which waved their heads in the torchlight and struggled when the hand gripped their backs to pinion their wings. Once the ring was on they were replaced on the ground, when they usually started an erratic half fluttering half falling rush over the boulders to the sea.

My opinion at a later date is that this particular group of birds were non breeding birds acting out for a year or two ahead, much as other species in their family who are also single egg long living birds such as the Fulmar Petrel. Hence the maritime urge and less inclination to dive down a hole.

At 01.45 hours we started on the cliff path, and having reached the top, ate our oranges. Then started the torchlit stumble towards home along the Glen Mor wall/bank with a faintly lit horizon to the NE.

Reaching the road we turned towards Decca. The Flannans' light flashed beyond Boreray. Ahead of us in the still air could be heard the chorus of Carn Mor's 'cousins' on Dun. Shearwaters called over there, and they had no nocturnal prowlers to disturb them. Our return at 02.45 hours was followed by a cup of tea and bed half an hour later.

The sun shone over Oiseval and soaked the bay in yellow light. How welcome. They were firing today so it was not a normal Sunday, and after seeing one or two sick, writing some notes, and having cocoa, Richard, the successor MO went around the village with me. At noon I returned and removed a sebaceous cyst from one of the civilian labourers, getting it out whole.

After lunch we both walked slowly up the road to the top. A gentle NE breeze blew onto the island, lifting over the cold north facing cliffs to form great white clouds which clung tenaciously to their creators, slinking around them as if shy of the peaks themselves. Soay was so capped and small clouds drifting up from Glen Bay, hurried to reach the top of the glen, mostly vanishing with the uprush of warm air from the sun warmed west cliffs. Outlying islands copied!

We returned down Glacan Conachair and were back by 16.45 hours. Although there is still abundant grass, the impression of decline in growth rate has become apparent during the last week. The heather is at its best and grass in seed is plentiful. Autumn tints appear and northern birds return. The year again turns towards its decline.

August 10

I showed Dr Richard Hudson how to change the drums on the thermohydrograph and barograph this morning and also did some work in the ration store. Later we did the cesspit together, and he was introduced to our fire fighting equipment. I have yet to teach him how to be a barber (and I don't mean barber surgeon).

As much as possible I have watched birds where conditions concentrate them, whether it be where food concentrates them such as on a lake or sewage farm, or where bad weather diverts them to a haven. The latter is to be expected in autumn when young birds wander without previous experience. Here we are subject to both types, but the impression is growing on me that here, though well placed to get transatlantic wanderers in the westerly winds, and overshooting birds around the 'top' of Scotland in easterly winds, some migrants use islands as intentional stopping posts.

Here White Wagtail, Snow Bunting and Meadow Pipit could come into this group as they regularly breed to the north of us.

August 11

Today should have been my last day in the Army (*I discovered later that according to regulations, from today I assume the rank of Major*). I handed the keys over to Richard. There is no likelihood of me getting off for five days and I have a job awaiting me in rural Herefordshire. The extra hours spent here are no burden.

August 12

A second fine day conducive to walking on the hills, which I did, walking with George, and returned stinking of Fulmar oil, which appropriately accompanied the sardines for supper.

August 13

Still in uniform. We heard this morning that eight people of officer status were expected on the *Mull* tomorrow night including Lord and Lady Tedder. Complete re-organisation of sleeping quarters will be needed. Most of the day was spent packing a suitcase but later I took a leisurely stroll up to the Gap, sitting on my favourite perch. A north easterly swell was coming in and I got home in time to give myself a haircut.

During the evening, having presented a barrel of beer to everyone caring to drink in MY canteen (or did it go with the keys), the sign of the PUFFINN watched its soon to leave painter right through to the end of a hilarious party until 03.00 hours, most of which we recorded to remind us in the morning of the eloquence and vocal aptitudes displayed by all. It was not blowing gale when I arose at 08.30 hours but was so by lunch time, the wind having been just north of east initially had now veered SE. This would cause the autumnal shifting of the sand so that there would be no sandy beach. Lord and Lady Tedder are no longer coming but surprisingly the *Mull* has only put off the sailing 24 hours. The depression deepens and I fear that the outlook is tinged with unjustifiable hope.

August 14

Blew hard all day. The *Mull*'s Skipper would be saying, 'I'll no' sail the noo.'

August 15

The wind had veered SSW overnight and the bay no longer had the full force of the heavy sea. The Spanish trawlers were now sheltering and spray was blowing across the bay, as I had remembered it did last autumn. The sandy beach now resides as a sandy bar with swirls of sand over it, 30 yards below the low tide 'line', its winter hide out.

August 16

Sunday. Yet again I had little hope of the *Mull* coming because of the state of the sea. However a higher barometric pressure and decaying winds gave hope for the morrow. A village walk in the afternoon was followed by a visit to the Gap. Stac Li had lost its bright whiteness as the brown young Gannets predominate over the white adults, many of which had shed parental cares. Usually at least one parent goes out on a long feeding trip in early morning, returning in the evening. There may then be a swap, but anyhow with more light in the evening, adults do the short trip to Village Bay to feed on the mackerel, who, being harried by the seals, break the surface as if striving to fly.

The Minch is a favourite feeding area and is available through the Sound of Harris 50 miles or around Barra head 100 miles. Radar observation a few days ago showed an average speed of 35mph.

Fulmars glided in front of me fresh from a summer moult, and birds shuffled on the ledges with mere traces of down. Their parents had gone off to moult, looking brownish with worn body feathers and with missing wing feathers, leaving them so fat that after their glide to the sea they will not be able to take off easily. Their ledge is then taken by a bird that had not yet bred, with feelings of 'first come first served', though this will be intermittent for several months.

I have heard tonight that the *Mull* intends to sail tomorrow. I really am prepared for this to be my last night here.

August 17

The weather reverted over night and wind, mist and rain persist this morning. It is very unlikely that she will sail in this and soon confirmation was forthcoming. Another village walk during the afternoon with nothing exiting and the hours drifted by unhitched by thoughts of action, and unhastened by the actions of others. The bracken is browning and thistles go mushy under foot. White Angelica that is tall enough escapes the sheep, and I feel that this is where I came in; head still as high as the Angelica and yet a feeling of impending autumn: a year to remember: a time to go.

Epilogue

....

St Kilda Wren

When I was 15 there were so few birdwatchers around that it was not a communal hobby, and this also applied to other branches of Natural History. So it was that my teenage attraction to islands, though centred around bird migration, developed and emerged, with a realisation that islands had virtues other than safe havens for migrants and breeding sites for sea birds. Fortunately there were others who thought like me, and while at Birmingham reading Medicine in the early 50s, a contemporary at Oundle School, David Hollands, had also retained Natural History, much of it out of hours, that we had been given *ex curriculo* as pupils.

We both kept daily diaries of our trips together; he continued his while preparing his books on Australian birds, and I as a rural GP took notes at lectures and on 'birdy' days. So my St Kilda Diaries were a habit. The invitation to publish them was accepted and with it the responsibility of conveying onto paper the unwritten sentiments experienced while trying to get the posting, getting it half promised, only getting two, extended to four, days warning, and never being told that there were additional non medical duties. My own mind was prepared for any medical or surgical situation and the bird/island position, but it was both wise and fortunate that I was a 'chap' tuned in to tough exercise that was neither combative or a contact sport.

However there was nothing that I was expected to do that could not be learnt from others, and on arrival it was clear that irrespective of rank or regiment we all had to learn from our fellows. It was really a combat zone without any bullets. The only communication we had with 'moms', girl friends, sick grannies, and best mates was by letters via sea (1 to 6 weeks) and the signallers, whose messages were vetted by security.

The only regrets we had at all levels were when carefully thought out requests to a high level as regards equipment were turned down or altered in a way that displayed ignorance of our role and location, and it sometimes took weeks to correct the mistake.

However this was my diary of duty work expected of me, of the work and activities that I took on, knowing I was capable of doing them, and worst of all the jobs, usually maritime, when I was in fear of mortal failure. Fortunately I enjoyed them all.

Long Tailed Field Mouse

David Boddington and Morton Boyd on Stac an Armin in 1959 (Scottish Natural Heritage)